# This Is a Very Important Lifetime for You

## Messages from Spirit

NANCY ADELE

*the Peppertree Press*
www.peppertreepublishing.com

Copyright © Nancy Adele, 2024

All rights reserved. Published by the Peppertree Press, LLC. the Peppertree Press and associated logos are trademarks of the Peppertree Press, LLC. No part of this publication may be reproduced, stored in a retrieval system, transmitted in any form or by any means, electronic, mechanical, photocopying, recording, or otherwise, without prior written permission of the publisher and author/illustrator. Graphic design by Elizabeth Parry.

For information regarding permission, call 941-922-2662 or contact us at our website: www.peppertreepublishing.com or write to:

The Peppertree Press, LLC. Attention: Publisher, 715 N. Washington Blvd., Suite B, Sarasota, Florida 34236

ISBN: 978-1-61493-960-3
Library of Congress: 2024911387
Printed: May 2024

Manufactured in the United States of America

# Dedication

**This book is dedicated to three beautiful Souls in Heaven and to Spirit.**

First, my daughter Kelsey Joy for assisting me in my spiritual awakening and guiding me on my journey.

Secondly, to my grandmother Adele who has been one of my main Spirit Guides.

Thirdly, to Deb Gniadek, thank you for your continued love and support, encouraging me to follow my Divine Path.

**Thank you to Spirit with humble gratitude for your ever-loving presence, guidance, and messages.**

# Acknowledgment

This book wouldn't be possible without the contribution of many. I'd like to begin by thanking my children Craig, Kelsey Joy, John Ryan and Caroline. Thank you for your loving hearts. Each of you means the world to me. Thank you to my Mom and Dad, especially my Dad who watches over me. A heartfelt gratitude to my sister Joy who joined me in making a dream come true opening our SoulfulWaves Wellness Center. Thank you to my brothers for being who you are. Thank you to many of my dear friends and all of those who joined me in this life's journey. Thank you to Mary Connors in Spirit and my good friend Maureen Ty who embraced my stories and took time to do the first-round edits. A very special thank you to Valerie Camozzi for her friendship, support throughout and helping me over countless hours to bring this book together. I am forever great~full.

THIS IS A VERY IMPORTANT LIFETIME FOR YOU

# Table of Contents

Introduction . . . . . . . . . . . . . . . . . . . . . . . . . . . . 1
Chapter 1. Kelsey Joy Angel ~ A Journey of Forgiveness . . . . . . . 3
Chapter 2: Delilah . . . . . . . . . . . . . . . . . . . . . . . . . . 9
Chapter 3: Dream of Warning . . . . . . . . . . . . . . . . . . . 12
Chapter 4: Let It Be . . . . . . . . . . . . . . . . . . . . . . . . 15
Chapter 5: Speaking to White Blood Cells . . . . . . . . . . . . 19
Chapter 6: 9-11, Kelsey Joy, and an Intuitive Student . . . . . . 22
Chapter 7: Ganesh and Lakshmi . . . . . . . . . . . . . . . . . . 25
Chapter 8: Sedona and The Rose Quartz Crystal . . . . . . . . . 27
Chapter 9: Sai Ma Opens the Energy of the
    Divine Mother . . . . . . . . . . . . . . . . . . . . . . . . . . 29
Chapter 10: The Womb . . . . . . . . . . . . . . . . . . . . . . . 34
Chapter 11: St. Joseph . . . . . . . . . . . . . . . . . . . . . . . . 36
Chapter 12: Fairies . . . . . . . . . . . . . . . . . . . . . . . . . . 39
Chapter 13: Ye Little Faith . . . . . . . . . . . . . . . . . . . . . 41
Chapter 14: Smells and Visions . . . . . . . . . . . . . . . . . . 43
Chapter 15: AMMA . . . . . . . . . . . . . . . . . . . . . . . . . 45
Chapter 16: Divinely Orchestrated . . . . . . . . . . . . . . . . 49
Chapter 17: My Native American Chief . . . . . . . . . . . . . 52
Chapter 18: Kwan Yin . . . . . . . . . . . . . . . . . . . . . . . . 54
Chapter 19: Sedona Healing Magic . . . . . . . . . . . . . . . . 57
Chapter 20: A Gift from Great Spirit . . . . . . . . . . . . . . . 61
Chapter 21: Durga~Divine Mother . . . . . . . . . . . . . . . . 63
Chapter 22: Wolf . . . . . . . . . . . . . . . . . . . . . . . . . . . 67
Chapter 23: Miracle Man . . . . . . . . . . . . . . . . . . . . . . 69
Chapter 24: Lucid Dreaming ~ *A Mermaid's Freedom
    from Bondage* . . . . . . . . . . . . . . . . . . . . . . . . . . 72

Chapter 25: A Lady in the Elevator . . . . . . . . . . . . . . . . . 74
Chapter 26: Ixchel . . . . . . . . . . . . . . . . . . . . . . . . . . . . . . 78
Chapter 27: Golden Statue . . . . . . . . . . . . . . . . . . . . . . . 87
Chapter 28: Sand Dollar I . . . . . . . . . . . . . . . . . . . . . . . . 91
Chapter 29: God Spoke to Me the Night
    Robin Williams Died . . . . . . . . . . . . . . . . . . . . . . . . 94
Chapter 30: Oliver . . . . . . . . . . . . . . . . . . . . . . . . . . . . . . 98
Chapter 31: The Healing of a Presidential Candidate . . . . . . 104
Chapter 32: Padre Pio . . . . . . . . . . . . . . . . . . . . . . . . . . 106
Chapter 33: The Shroud . . . . . . . . . . . . . . . . . . . . . . . . 111
Chapter 34: Padre Pio's Relics and the Walkway . . . . . . . . 114
Chapter 35: A Girl in Her Bright Yellow Plane . . . . . . . . . . 117
Chapter 36: Sand Dollar II . . . . . . . . . . . . . . . . . . . . . . . 123
Chapter 37: A Shaman, My Dad, and Sophia . . . . . . . . . . . 125
Chapter 38: Past Life in Athens, Greece . . . . . . . . . . . . . . 128
Chapter 39: Blue Avians . . . . . . . . . . . . . . . . . . . . . . . . 130
Chapter 40: Della Plant Spirit's Message . . . . . . . . . . . . . 132
Chapter 41: Mercury in Retrograde and
    Monument Valley . . . . . . . . . . . . . . . . . . . . . . . . . 134
Chapter 42: Spirit Appearing in My Room . . . . . . . . . . . . 138
Chapter 43: 2 ETs in My Back Seat . . . . . . . . . . . . . . . . . 141
Chapter 44: My White Jeep . . . . . . . . . . . . . . . . . . . . . . 143
Chapter 45: Archangel Michael, Blue Angels,
    and a Visit with Bigfoot . . . . . . . . . . . . . . . . . . . . 147
Chapter 46: Tall Gray Stone Beings . . . . . . . . . . . . . . . . . 152
Chapter 47: A School Teacher, a Student,
    and a Tornado . . . . . . . . . . . . . . . . . . . . . . . . . . . 156
About the Author . . . . . . . . . . . . . . . . . . . . . . . . . . . . 160

# INTRODUCTION

My book begins with a major loss. Through this loss I still had to show up for my family and work, leaving little time to grieve. During this time, I experienced miracles and messages from Spirit. While going through my divorce I was disheartened for my children and myself. I continued to have experiences that helped me to heal and to remember who I truly am. I was on a healing journey which took me to different places and sacred sites. Spirit guided me throughout my journey helping me to create an enriched life. There were good times and bad times though once I understood the messages I was receiving, I began to see light on my path.

Spirit continuously lit my path through life's ups and downs. In every tragedy or trauma there is a silver lining. We may not see it while going through it, however, when we find it, our healing emerges.

Writing this book reminded me of all the blessings I have received throughout my life. My hope is through reading this book that you will recognize the synchronicities, messages, and blessings in your life.

# CHAPTER 1

# Kelsey Joy Angel – A Journey of Forgiveness

I was married very young. I think it's what I thought I was supposed to do. Marriage was the next step in a young woman's life. Marriage, children, and I'm not sure what after that. I am a nurse, a new mother with another baby on the way, but I still felt there was so much more for me to explore.

I was 37 and 1/2 weeks pregnant when my water broke. This baby was coming into the world. I knew in my heart she would be a girl and her name would be Kelsey Joy. We went to the hospital and I was admitted promptly by my primary obstetrician.

After my examination, he started me on a drug called Pitocin to help with the contractions. I had been there for several hours, when at midnight a change of shift occurred. The other obstetrician of that practice came into my room. I had seen him a few times at the office, but I didn't care for his arrogance.

After examining me, he decided to discharge me and send me home, because I wasn't further along in labor. He said I was leaking amniotic fluid. However, although it was a high leak, my baby's head wasn't far enough down to keep me in the hospital. The obstetrician did not believe my water had fully broken; it had. I felt disbelief, but he refused to listen and discharged me.

I went home feeling angry, disappointed, and dismayed. It was difficult accepting such a situation with these intense feelings. Pushing my emotions aside, I kept trying to convince myself that the obstetrician had to know what he was doing—after all it was his field of practice.

It had been over a week since I had been discharged. I went to my next scheduled appointment with my primary obstetrician that week. Afterwards, I felt strange that I didn't feel any movement of the baby. When I couldn't feel her, I panicked and immediately drove myself to the hospital for an emergency ultrasound.

I took one look at the ultrasound technician's face and knew something terrible had occurred. She rushed out of the room to get the doctor. The doctor used his stethoscope to hear my baby's heartbeat, but could not detect one.

I couldn't believe what they were saying. I was in a state of shock. When I received this devastating news, I was by myself, but my husband arrived at the hospital later. We looked at each other in disbelief.

I cried out, "Our baby can't be dead!"

Then I was told that I still had to deliver my baby. Once again, they induced my labor with Pitocin. During this whole agonizing period, I prayed that the doctors were wrong. Perhaps that was delusional, but I hoped and prayed that my baby was still alive.

After twenty-four long, painful hours, I finally delivered my beautiful baby girl. She was stillborn, with no signs of life. Kelsey was 9 pounds, 13 ounces, perfect in every way, and looked like my son.

Since I had lost a lot of blood, I had to be monitored closely. I was also emotionally distraught at our loss of this beautiful perfect infant. I had so many unanswered questions. Why did they send me home too early? Why couldn't they have done a C-Section? Why couldn't they have protected my unborn child?

# THIS IS A VERY IMPORTANT LIFETIME FOR YOU

It was an awful, devastating time to go through. I was fortunate that I had amazing nurses caring for me. They encouraged me to hold my little girl and to have pictures taken while I held her. My nurse said that later I would want the pictures, so I did. It seemed like everything was just a blur.

I was so numb, I didn't even know what was happening. I had carried this precious infant of mine for nine months in anticipation of a life with her and a future seeing her grow up, only to have her to be born lifeless. No one is *ever* prepared for this.

It was a sad scene when my father came into the room to see her. I had never seen my dad cry. He sobbed openly and couldn't contain himself. My family was encouraged to hold Kelsey and I felt I had to be the strong one supporting each of them.

When my very sensitive and quiet brother held her, I noticed blood was trickling down Kelsey's nose. I knew this was scary for him. My response was to protect him, so I told him not to worry about it, as I gently wiped the blood away. This was all so surreal.

They transferred me to the post-partum floor with the other mothers, with their living babies. I could hear those crying babies, but I was all alone. I was grieving, without my precious baby girl. I had to leave the hospital without my beautiful baby in my arms.

There were whispers among family members that the arrogant doctor who had been on call for the practice was incompetent. He should have kept me at the hospital when my water broke. I should not have been sent home, but I couldn't think about it.

Two weeks later I made an appointment to talk with my primary obstetrician, the one I liked and who had followed my prenatal care. He was the doctor I trusted. He is also the one who believed me when I told him my water broke—the one who had admitted me to the hospital.

His response to this tragedy and the death of my baby was unreal, as all he said was, "We all make mistakes."

I was shocked at his response. This was pure negligence on the part of that arrogant obstetrician and an inappropriate response from my primary caregiver. It isn't okay for doctors not to be held accountable for gross medical errors.

We hired a lawyer, but quickly learned that doctors don't testify against other doctors. This was tough to hear. Now I had to learn one of the biggest lessons of my life—forgiveness. I had to forgive that arrogant doctor who took our baby's life from us.

I visited Kelsey's gravesite every day. My poor son was only a year-and-a-half old and his mother was a grieving woman. I tried my best to put on a happy face around him.

My grief was overflowing. It was Easter weekend and my mother begged me to come to the Cape for a change of scenery. I told her I couldn't go, because I still needed to visit Kelsey's gravesite. My mother said, "It's OK. You could miss a day of not going."

My response to her was, "Kelsey is not at the Cape." I was conflicted about going, but I reluctantly decided to go anyway.

Later, while at my parent's house, I had my son in my arms and went out on the deck to get some fresh air. When I looked up in the sky, I saw a divine cloud formation of a perfect angel. It was the sign I needed. Kelsey, my beautiful angel, sent me a sign. I could breathe—I could breathe again.

Much later in a conversation with my sister, Joy, she told me she had a dream prior to Kelsey's death. In the dream, my sister said that she had died. To honor her, I named my baby, Joy Kelsey. Looking back, what I realized was that without us knowing, Joy's dream was preparing us for Kelsey's passing.

As I went through the stages of grief, it took a couple of years for me to recover. I was receiving subtle signs from Spirit on my

THIS IS A VERY IMPORTANT LIFETIME FOR YOU

healing journey. I felt hopeful as the layers of deep sadness were beginning to lift. I kept Kelsey Joy close to my heart.

I sensed that things were beginning to look up, so that I was contemplating conceiving again. Kelsey Joy will always be an integral part of me. However, before becoming pregnant again, we went to a high-risk obstetrician. We wanted to make sure it was safe for us to have another child after the loss of Kelsey Joy. The obstetrician requested Kelsey's autopsy results.

When she discussed this with us, she confirmed my suspicion that my daughter had died from Cytomegalovirus. This was an infection that occurred when my water broke and I was sent home by that arrogant doctor.

She went on to say that it was fortunate I survived. That was the moment I realized my daughter was watching over me. She was *my* angel.

My pregnancy with my second son went well. The plan was to deliver him a week early, because it was discovered at my appointment that he was a breech baby. They decided to turn him to the correct position in the doctor's office, but that was unsuccessful.

When I left the office, intense discomfort made me drop to my knees. The baby had reverted to the breech position. A week later I delivered a beautiful healthy boy. My faith was restored, and I once again was blessed. Thank you, God.

It wasn't until much later that I realized Kelsey Joy was the catalyst for my spiritual awakening. I could have curled up and held onto my anger and all that comes with it, but I didn't. I was living my life again.

Over time, I realized it was all in Divine Order. As difficult for some to believe, even myself at times, I wouldn't change a thing. I am who I am, because of it. On this journey of awakening, I was shown I had several past lives where I lost a baby. What I

7

found was that I just didn't learn the lessons that I was trying to teach myself in those lifetimes. I let anger, resentment, guilt, and shame control me.

In my subsequent pregnancies in this life, I learned to speak up. If one person did not listen to my concerns, I knew another one would. I also learned the power of forgiveness. I continue to learn ways of trusting my intuition, as I navigate through this lifetime.

Did this doctor purposely want to hurt my baby? I don't believe he did. I know he has his own life lessons to learn, and I pray that he does, for the sake of his patients.

> The silver lining to this was the empowerment for me to forgive myself and others. We may not see it immediately, but there is always light in the presence of darkness.

# CHAPTER 2

# Delilah

It is 5 a.m. August 1990. I am waking to the phone ringing. Who would be calling at this time?

I answered the phone, only to hear my mother, apologizing for the early call. She said, "I know you've had a tough year, but I have to tell you some bad news."

The tough year to which my mother was referring is that I lost my baby in February. My mother then proceeded to say that our family friend, Delilah, had died. "She's okay," came immediately out of my mouth.

My mother exclaimed, "What?"

I said, "She's okay. Delilah came to me in a dream last night." Then I proceeded to share my dream with my mom. I knew it was a visitation from Delilah.

I told her, "I was getting onto a bus, but there was only one passenger on it. It was a girl, she had the back of her head facing me. Yet I knew it was Delilah, because I could see her wavy hair. As I walked down the bus aisle, she turned around and with a beautiful smile said, "Tell them I'm okay."

The next thing I knew was that I was standing outside a Floridian front door. I recognized this type of door, because Mom and Dad have one in their Florida home.

Mom said, "I didn't know you knew that Delilah moved to Florida two weeks ago."

I told my mom I didn't know that. Then I continued to describe my very vivid dream to her.

Delilah's dad opened the door and embarrassingly said, "Oh, Nancy," as he was standing there in his boxer shorts.

"Oh, Mr. Henry!"

He immediately ran into the living room and sat down on a pull-out couch. It was puzzling to me, because he seemed like he was visiting someone and that this wasn't his house.

I told my mom that the dream shifted and now I was standing in the middle of the foyer, a tile floor under my feet, and stairs across from me, but now Mr. Henry and Delilah's sister were also there. It seemed strange that the ceiling was falling all around us. I knew something tragic had just happened and then, Mom, you called me.

My mother said, "You really didn't know that Delilah had moved to Florida?"

I said, "I had no idea." I hadn't seen Delilah since high school.

Delilah was one year behind me, but our mothers were very close friends. When I was little, I would go with my mother when she visited them. Both of our mothers were into dogs and the garden club.

My mother then proceeded to tell me that Delilah had been going to an interview, but her car was hit by a huge truck. When the truck rolled over, it ended up rolling over her car, too. She died instantly.

"Oh, no!" I exclaimed.

My mom said she was going to see Delilah's mother tomorrow, I asked her to please tell them that Delilah had come to me in a dream and said she was okay.

The next evening, I received another phone call from my mother. She said, "Nancy, I told Delilah's mom about your dream. We were sitting across from each other in the kitchen when I began telling her about your dream. After I told her the part about you seeing her husband opening the door, guess who came into the kitchen in his boxer shorts? Mr. Henry! We both screamed!"

He didn't know I was there at the house, so he thought we were screaming because he was undressed. Later he found out it was because of my dream. But how did I know that he wore boxer shorts?

Over the years, Delilah came to me many times with the same message for her mother. She kept telling me that she was worried about her mother and to let her know that she was okay. I would call her each time Delilah came through to me. Her mother would say thank you and tell me that she heard this same message from others, but told me she couldn't get past the loss of her beloved daughter.

---

> Delilah's messages helped me to let go of my own grief, as a mother losing my baby. Even though I received my own messages that my baby, Kelsey, who passed over, is well cared for, I found these messages to be very comforting. Messages like this are usually for many of us at the same time.

---

## CHAPTER 3

# Dream of Warning

In dreamtime, I was driving on 128 south in the second lane over from the fast lane. I recognized it in this dream, because I drove this way home from work every evening. It was pitch black and I was completely stopped on the highway in the lane next to the fast lane. I was parked on a highway, in our van and my lights are out. Oh my!

This was a recurring dream I have had for months. I woke up every time in panic and fear. I tried to go back to sleep, but it was never easy. Normally; I would wake up, because I have a newborn in the house. Sleep wasn't a commodity. With sleep deprivation, I just wanted a good night's sleep.

One evening I was at work and we were all telling stories at the nurses' station. Most of our patients had gone to bed and our evening tasks were pretty much done. We sat between two units and talked about angels, near-death experiences, and all that fascinating stuff. Most of us believed in angels and signs—I know I did.

It was 11:30 at night when our shift was over. We walked to our cars and began our way home. I was driving down the side road—a road I knew very well. I remembered when I found out I was having another girl. I knew it before we were even told, because of signs.

# THIS IS A VERY IMPORTANT LIFETIME FOR YOU

One night as I came out of work, I looked up into the tree to see a Mylar balloon stuck there. The balloon that was caught in the tree proclaimed, "It's a girl!"

On that same evening with the balloon, I was driving on this road and the only sign that was lit said, "Caroline." Prior to knowing the gender of my baby, I had picked the name Caroline. I never thought of a boy's name. Again, these are signs.

As usual, the road was dark. I drove as I always did, but somehow this felt different. An overwhelming feeling of despair started to creep over me. I didn't know what was happening, so I started to panic. I couldn't breathe, but I didn't know why I was feeling this way. I just had an overwhelming feeling of doom and gloom that I couldn't shake. I thought I was going to die that night.

I need to get home to my children, and to my baby. God, please help me! Angels, please help me! Protect me, as I need to get home to my children. My children need their mother.

I wept as I was driving. To many, it was just another night, but to me it felt like my last night on earth. I continued to drive on this curvy side road and gradually made my way out to the highway. I started gathering up speed, but once I was going about 60 mph, I moved over into the second lane. It was dark, but not many cars were on the road at this hour.

I couldn't stop crying, so I tried to focus on the road. That's when I saw it. Up in front of me was a van with its lights out, just sitting in my lane. Oh God! I was going too fast; I forcefully gripped the steering wheel and pulled it completely to the left and then a quick right. I swerved left into the other lane, but I didn't have time to look. I just did it and swerved back, once I felt I had cleared this van.

"Oh my God!" I sobbed and sobbed all the way home. I was shaking, as I now knew what the dream or nightmare was—it was warning me. It wasn't my van stopped on the highway, but it was another van. *Thank you, God.*

---

Thank you, Angels, for warning and saving me, even though I didn't know it at the time. This was one night I couldn't get home fast enough to hug my children. For I knew I was saved that night.

---

## CHAPTER 4

# Let It Be

At this time, my sweet daughter is eight months old and my sons are three and seven years old. My parents are visiting from out of town, and we are all huddled around the television with palpable tension in the air.

"When are they going to announce it?" We were waiting and it seemed like forever. We are finally going to hear the verdict of one of the most notable murder cases: the trial of OJ Simpson for the gruesome death of his wife, Nicole Brown Simpson, and Ron Goldman. This case consumed much of our lives.

For months and months, day after day, that's all you would see on TV. The poor woman—have we forgotten her horrendous death? I am going to be so happy when this is over or so I thought. The verdict was not guilty.

What, how can this be? We know he's guilty. He knows it, we all know it. I can't believe what I am hearing and seeing. This is an example of what money and celebrity status can do. I just wanted to reach through the television and have him feel the pain and trauma he inflicted on his wife.

Where is the justice? How can this be? I could feel my blood pressure rising. I started feeling panicky and extremely hot. My parents were talking about the verdict and even yelling. They are very passionate people when it comes to certain things and viewpoints. Today was no exception.

My emotions were building. I had to get out of the house now. I quickly asked if they could watch the kids and flew out the door. I have pictures that need to be picked up, so I quickly yell back into the house, "I'm going to the photo shop, I'll be right back."

Making my way through the shop door, I see there's a line, but that's okay—I can deal with it. Time to chill is good for me right now and this is an opportunity. I will be okay. I even breathed a little fresh air while driving to the shop and was able to regain my composure.

Well, that was short-lived. I noticed a television behind the counter. The OJ Simpson verdict is still all over the news. Who is this woman standing right in front of me? She opens her mouth and starts cheering. I could see her face, filled with joy, and not having any problems expressing it. Her excitement was due to OJ Simpson's "Not Guilty" verdict. Okay, fine, everyone has a right to their own opinion. Just don't push it onto everyone—this is one of my biggest pet peeves.

Having our own experiences and opinions is one of the wonderful things about being human, I had thought, up until this day. This woman in line didn't hold back and she let everyone know. She didn't care if OJ murdered his wife, Nicole, and Ron or not. She just wanted him acquitted.

What, are you kidding? It was her lack of understanding of the gravity of the situation that was getting to me. She didn't care if he was guilty or not.

I felt rage once again. I didn't want to be here in the store. If I stay, I will let this woman know exactly how I feel. Once I open my mouth, there's no holding back at this point.

This isn't good, so I need to get out of here. Air, I just need air, but once I open my mouth … I stormed out without my photos. I felt like I was going to burst. I started driving around, trying to clear my head, and eventually pulled into my driveway.

I knew my parents needed to leave to go home. They left shortly after I returned. My thoughts were to get through the remainder of the evening, but I just wanted to go to bed, pull the covers up over my head, and cry.

Once I got the kids to bed, I crawled into bed myself. I'm feeling completely defeated and depleted. I thought, *What's the use? There is no justice. How could this be?*

When I think about it, anger just consumes me. I must stop mulling over it, especially the way that woman in the store was cheering when she heard the verdict. Filled with exhaustion, I fell asleep right away that night. This was my pattern—to work all day, put the kids to bed, and fall into a deep sleep, but then to wake up at 3 a.m.

This night was no different, except for one thing—I woke up to the presence of Mother Mary. What an indescribable feeling, like holding a precious child for the first time. I don't remember feeling *this* much unconditional love and peace flowing through my being.

At this moment, *I am the child* and my mother is enveloping me in her arms, with complete love and protection. I see Mother Mary now standing in the corner of my room. She was still, looking more like a statue, with her head lowered to one side in reverence.

Behind Mother Mary was a stained glass window like you would see in a church. Streaming through the church-like window is a beautiful blue, green, and violet light shining into the room. She exudes pure love.

I felt such peace, like I was floating, drifting like on the beautiful blue serene ocean. All my anger was gone. Everything was washed away. I am calm, lying here, feeling so peaceful.

Mother Mary says to me, "Don't let this be the instance that separates people. Let it be—it's just a blip in time." I realized that it's not that Nicole's or Ron's life didn't matter, but this outcome should not create such a devastating division and separation of humanity.

> The lesson was to bring a message of peace: to demonstrate the importance of continuing to be loving of one another, regardless of color, race, religion, or gender. It doesn't matter. We are all ONE.

When I woke up, I was filled with love and understanding. I knew there was something much deeper being presented to me. While in the midst of the anger and chaos, I couldn't comprehend the enormity of what was truly happening, but I am forever changed. Paul McCartney had it right, when he wrote the song, *Let it Be*. "Mother Mary, speaking words of wisdom, let it be."

# CHAPTER 5

# Speaking to White Blood Cells

This story begins with one of my best friends calling me to share that she was diagnosed with Stage 3 breast cancer. This news was devastating, as she already was barely coping, because she was going through a very difficult divorce. After hearing the news, I began meeting with her every week to give her Reiki sessions, which continued for over a year.

Several months into her treatment, my friend planned a trip to Disney World with her children during school vacation. They loved Disney World and this would be a nice break during a stressful time. Each week when I saw her for Reiki, she excitedly talked about her upcoming trip. I hadn't seen her light up like this for a very long time.

Their trip was less than a week away when my friend called again. She sounded upset on the phone. She had just left her doctor's appointment, and she proceeded to tell me that her doctor said she couldn't go on her trip. The doctor advised her against traveling and told her that the chemotherapy had lowered her white blood cell count.

She begged the doctor to allow her to go. My friend is a nurse practitioner and one of the smartest people I know. She knew it would be risky, because her immune system was compromised, but she felt strongly that her family would benefit from this trip.

My friend asked her doctor a very important question. She asked if her white blood cell count increased by Friday, would it be safe for her to travel. Friday was only four days away, so her doctor looked at her in disbelief. The doctor knew my friend was a nurse practitioner and wondered why she would ask this, but told her she could travel if her blood work showed improvement.

My friend suspected her doctor was just saying *yes* to appease her, so she asked her what white blood cell range would be acceptable for her to be able to go. After her doctor gave her a range, she called me to explain what they discussed. She said to me, "Nancy, we need to get my white blood cell count up by Friday and you're going to help me do it."

I responded with, "Okay I'm in."

Everything was now in motion. My friend decided to focus on an acceptable white blood cell count number. I knew the more specific we were, the easier it would be for my friend to accomplish and manifest it.

While on the phone together, we put out to the Universe in spoken words that my friend and her children were going to Disney and wanted to have a great trip. She spoke the number out loud that she decided her white blood cell count would be. I encouraged her to write down that number on sticky notes and put the notes everywhere. She put them in her car, on her refrigerator, on her cabinets, her nightstands, and in every room in her house.

In addition, we created a positive affirmation together for her to repeat.

I encouraged her to visualize her white blood cells like rabbits, multiplying and multiplying. I also spoke the words and affirmed this for her. In addition, whenever she had a moment, I suggested

# THIS IS A VERY IMPORTANT LIFETIME FOR YOU

she visualize herself in detail at Disney World with her children. We both would repeat over and over her affirmation, with the feeling of being there, as if it already existed. She continued to do this daily.

My friend called me Friday morning and said her blood had been drawn. When her doctor entered the room with her chart, she was shaking her head in disbelief. My friend said the expression on her doctor's face was priceless. Her doctor proceeded to say she didn't know what my friend did, but her white blood cell count was high enough to go to Disney World with her family. She was very excited and thanked her doctor profusely.

With curiosity she asked her doctor, "What was my white blood cell count?"

Her doctor looked at her, as if to ask, why does it matter. As it turned out, the result was the exact number we both had been saying and visualizing over the past four days. Her doctor asked how she did it, so my friend shared what we had been doing. Her doctor was amazed.

Personally, I was, too. I know we are co-creators, divine beings here on earth with infinite capabilities. This felt more like a miracle to all of us. My friend and her children went on their trip to Disney World and had a wonderful time. Today my friend is cancer-free.

> She shares her experience with all those who cross her path and those in need of encouragement as they travel their own journey. We both share her story in hopes of uplifting others. Thank you, Infinite Creator, for showing us that we are not alone.

# CHAPTER 6

# 9-11, Kelsey Joy, and an Intuitive Student

It was September 11, 2001, and I was driving to meet my Reiki friend on the South Shore. It was my day off from work at the school. My Reiki friend and I had been trying to get together to do a Qigong meditation by the water near her house. We finally made plans for today, so I was on my way to meet her.

As I was driving, I heard a voice—it was my daughter, Kelsey Joy, in Spirit. She urged me to turn on the radio. I heard, "Turn the radio on, turn it on!" I immediately put the radio on and heard the news of a plane crashing into one of the Twin Towers in New York. I couldn't believe what I was hearing. I started to cry and began shaking, but I continued driving and praying, weeping as I drove.

When I arrived at my friend's house, she came running out to the car and told me that a second plane had crashed into the Twin Towers.

We were both shaken, but felt we needed to do a healing meditation and Qigong more than ever. However, first I had to check in on my children, who were in school. I had difficulty getting through on the phone, but I'm sure everyone was calling at the same time.

We finally left to walk down to the water as I continued to call. Once I was able to get through, I let them know that I'd be picking them up immediately. My Reiki friend and I did our healing meditation, sending healing energy out to all involved and to the world.

We didn't stay much longer at the water, so I could leave quickly. I headed straight to my children. I think most people felt the same way that day and acted as I did, too. We needed to have our loved ones close at heart. It was also important to call and tell family and friends how much we loved them. Life is too short, especially on a day like today.

It was a difficult night trying to explain to our children what *may* have happened, while reassuring them that they were safe. The next morning, I was back to work at the nursing office at school. When I walked in, I couldn't believe my eyes. On our whiteboard, someone had drawn two tall buildings with two planes headed towards the buildings.

I asked the other nurse with whom I worked about the drawings. She said she hadn't noticed the drawing until I mentioned it. She went on to explain that on Monday, an elementary student was ill and while waiting for his mom to pick him up, he must have drawn on the whiteboard. She said she never paid attention. The drawing was done the day *before* the attack of 9/11. That student who went home on Monday was very intuitive.

I wondered if he knew what was going to happen and this made him feel ill. I reached out to his counselor to share what had happened. She was going to call his mom to see how he was feeling. The counselor said she wasn't surprised about the student's drawing, because she felt this student was very sensitive. This was a difficult time for everyone dealing with the tragedy that had occurred.

I thanked my beautiful Kelsey Joy angel for alerting me to what was happening. It was comforting to know she's watching over us. I sense her around me and feel her touch when she caresses the right side of my forehead, but this was the first time I heard her sweet, yet forceful voice.
I am forever great~full.

# CHAPTER 7

# Ganesh and Lakshmi

I was brought up Catholic, but I was drawn to and intrigued by Hinduism. Something drew me to pictures and images of Hindu Goddesses and Gods. Early in my spiritual awakening, I experienced guidance from the Hindu God/Goddess deities. I didn't know how truly I was connected to them.

As a young child, I vividly remember having a dream about being in a cave, sitting on a granite bench with an elephant-headed boy. He talked with me for a while, but upon waking, I didn't remember most of what he said to me with the exception of the statement, "Radha is Love."

Later, in my thirties, recollecting these childhood dreams, I realized who this was—Ganesh, the remover of obstacles. I began reading about him and learned that he didn't allow many people in his cave. What? I didn't know he lived in a cave. Wow, this is so cool.

To this day, he guides me. I call upon him, especially when there's something I need to release. One vivid experience I had was in a lucid dream. Ganesh had his third eye up to my third eye. I could see peripherally his physical eyes way out to the sides. He was large and violet in color, decorated with crystals and jewels. It was truly amazing! I received the message that Ganesh was opening my third eye.

When I think of Ganesh, I often think of Lakshmi, too. They work together. She is a beautiful Hindu Goddess. I wasn't aware of my connection with Lakshmi, until I took my first "Angel Messenger" class. Part of our homework assignment was to practice working with a deity. I wasn't sure who to choose, so I picked a Goddess Card, which was Green Tara.

As I drove home, my intention was to work with her until our next class. However, that was not what Spirit had in mind! It was the same night, and all night, I heard this voice—yes, outside my head! It kept calling, "Lakshmi, Lakshmi, Lakshmi," continuously. I didn't get much sleep.

When I shared the experience with a couple of friends, they asked if I felt frightened. I said no, because I just knew that I was to be working with Lakshmi, the Goddess of bright futures and abundance.

Over the next couple of weeks, Lakshmi spoke again. I heard, "Tantra, Tantra, Tantra," and "Rolfing, Rolfing, Rolfing." I would meditate after hearing her messages to receive more guidance.

*Clairaudience* means clear hearing. This hadn't been my strongest intuitive sense, but I heard her messages very clearly. To this day, I know Ganesh and Lakshmi are with me, assisting and guiding me in my life. Anyone can call on them for assistance in their life. Hindu deities are omnipresent and help many. When calling on them to help, be sure to command for your highest good and the highest good of all.

CHAPTER 8

# Sedona and the Rose Quartz Crystal

I was attending a retreat to Sedona with my Reiki teacher. It was my first trip to Sedona. I never thought I would like the desert, because I'm a Pisces, a water girl. I remember going for a reading in Boston, prior to booking my trip to Sedona. The psychic said, "I see you in the desert."

I responded, "What?"

He said, "You will love it there."

There were six of us altogether. Our Reiki teacher had rented a van to take us from the airport for our stay in Sedona. We planned to visit many sacred sites in Sedona.

I was very excited. As we were getting closer to the Sedona exit, my hands started shaking uncontrollably. It was the energy and I felt it immediately. As we drove along 179 near the artist area of Tlaquepaque, I pointed to places to which I had traveled in my dreams the night before. It was surreal.

We arrived at our hotel and started checking in. I was sharing a room with a woman who had just been diagnosed with breast cancer. After we settled in our rooms, our Reiki teacher informed us we would be heading down to Cathedral Rock for the afternoon. I heard that it was amazing there.

As we exited the van, I looked up and saw the most beautiful view of Red Rock. Seeing this formation in a photograph is one thing, but in person is absolutely another. It was truly spectacular there.

We all proceeded to walk down to the creek, where we were instructed to find a spot to meditate. I found my spot next to the creek. It was a perfect place to lay my small crystals in the water to be cleansed.

During meditation, I received a clear message from my guides to give the woman with whom I was sharing a room the pink rose quartz crystal. I got up, went over to her, and shared with her that I was guided to give this rose quartz crystal to her.

She immediately thanked me, took the pink rose crystal, and put it into her bra. She told me that she had recently been diagnosed with a breast tumor. I thought that she had chosen an excellent spot to put it.

The next morning, my friend came out of the bathroom after getting dressed. She asked me if I wanted to see my crystal. I told her that it wasn't mine, because I gave it to her.

She put the crystal into my hand and to my complete surprise, the pink rose quartz was no longer pink—it was totally clear! Where did the pink go? I intuitively received the message that she had absorbed all the pink healing color into her body.

> This was a first for me—I've never heard of this happening before. However, all things are possible within the Universe. Thank you, Spirit and the Universe, for the alignment with my roommate and the rose quartz crystal.

CHAPTER 9

# Sai Ma Opens the Energy of the Divine Mother

Time is very different in Spirit. It's not linear like our present physical time. Looking back, it was truly Sai Ma who clearly opened the energy of Divine Mother after my experience with Mary. The beginning of this story is my introduction to Sai Baba.

It was summertime and I was driving, listening to an audiobook, *The Power of Intention* by Wayne Dyer. I consider this to be his best book. One section in it talks about an Avatar in India named Sai Baba. As I listened about Sai Baba, I prayed to him to help me have a deeper connection with the Divine Mother.

Later that day, I drove to Cape Cod to see my parents. When I arrived, my mother asked if I wanted to go to the second-hand bookstore. I love books, so that was an invitation I wasn't going to pass up. It was a small store, not well organized, but I can always find the metaphysical or New Age section.

As I was walking by one of those sections, I heard a book drop behind me. I looked back to see if I had bumped something. There on the floor was a book entitled. *Sai Baba.*

Are you kidding? The Universe was listening to my thoughts. I couldn't believe my eyes! I bought the book and later told my mother the story. She's intuitive and found it pretty amazing. I was meant to read this book. I found a section in the book with prayers one can say to Sai Baba.

A few months earlier I had taken a trip to Sedona with my Reiki group. Anyone who has visited Sedona is aware that magical stuff happens. This time, the magic occurred not in Sedona, but after my return home. I had been contemplating a divorce for some time, as we had simply been growing apart, which began shortly after my first child was born.

I worked ten-hour days, which left little time to be with my children. I couldn't leave my job, because I was the main support of my family. Early one morning, around 4 a.m., I woke up in bed to see a woman sitting at the foot of our bed. This wasn't in dreamtime, as she looked like she was physically present. However, I wasn't scared.

She was sitting on my side of the bed. She had short jet-black hair, was dressed in purple, and had her back to me. I felt love emanating from her. I became calm and peaceful. I laid my head down on the pillow, but when I turned to look again, she was gone.

I was perplexed, because she had her back to me. Wondering who this woman was, I thought maybe she was my spirit guide.

By October of that same year, it was time to ask for a divorce—not a separation. I knew our marriage was over. I had tried very hard to make things work, but I was exhausted.

One of my Reiki friends called to say that there was a woman from India known as a Divine Mother, who was coming to speak at a hotel nearby that night. I was invited to attend this event with my friend.

When we arrived, most of the attendees were dressed in saris. We found our seats toward the back. The energy in the room felt palpable. An empty chair draped in gold with a white outfit and

# THIS IS A VERY IMPORTANT LIFETIME FOR YOU

gold sandals was onstage. The room was buzzing with chatter.

Since the Divine Mother was about to make her entrance, it was time for everyone to be quiet. A beautiful woman dressed in a purple silk gown appeared onstage. Her presence and energy felt Divine.

This woman was introduced as Sai Ma. She took her seat next to the empty one draped in gold. She explained that the chair next to her was to honor her Guru, Sai Baba.

Sai Ma spoke about divine love and spiritual awakening. She asked why people came that night and called upon the audience to share why they came. I never do this, but I felt compelled to stand up and speak.

When it was my turn, she asked me why I had come. I said my friends informed me of this event and I wanted to see what it was about.

Then she said to me, *"This is a very important lifetime for you."* It was as if she knew my soul.

I didn't think anything of it, until at 3:30 a.m., I woke up. I realized that she was the woman with her back to me, who had been sitting on my bed. I sobbed, but I didn't say anything to my husband that morning. I had to get up and go to work. I wasn't sure how I could make it through the day. I couldn't believe it was her. What is happening?

I finally left for work, though had to leave as I suddenly felt ill. I decided to go back to the hotel where Sai Ma was teaching a workshop. However, when I arrived, there wasn't anyone in the welcoming area and the doors were closed to the conference room.

I couldn't hold my tears back any longer, as I had this intense feeling that I needed to see her once again. A few minutes later, a woman in a white sari came out and asked if she could help me.

I told her I needed to see Sai Ma. She said it wasn't possible right now, since she was teaching a workshop.

I said, "You don't understand. Sai Ma was sitting on my bed a few months ago."

The woman said, "Oh, yes, she does that."

My emotions overcame me, and I began to cry again. The woman was very kind. She said that I could go into the workshop for half a day, so I went in and sat down. Sai Ma was in town for four days. I went back each evening while she was in town.

One evening she called me onto the stage. Sai Ma spoke to me personally about my life. She could visualize my current life, while emphasizing this lifetime is about me—not about my husband or anyone else.

She knew about my current situation, without me telling her that I was contemplating a divorce. Sai Ma spoke to me about taking my time and not to rush into anything.

This was confirmation that I could tell my husband when *I* was ready. It was OK to wait until after the holidays. My husband thought I would change my mind about leaving, because I had done this a few times in the past. However, I was done trying everything under the sun to make things work out for our children. I could not do it this time, as I was dying inside and needed to save myself.

My experience with Sai Ma and Sai Baba during this volatile time in my life was helpful and imprinted me energetically. The words that Sai Ma spoke to me, *"It's a very important lifetime for you,"* stayed with me long after the workshop was over.

I returned home that night once the workshop concluded with a deep realization that my life purpose would involve making changes in my life, of which this divorce would be a part. I felt hope knowing my new beginnings were within reach.

THIS IS A VERY IMPORTANT LIFETIME FOR YOU

I am great~full for the divine synchronicities that brought both Sai Ma and Sai Baba into my life.

## CHAPTER 10

# The Womb

My dream state brought me to my womb where my spirit guide appeared. He revealed another aspect of me. It was as if I was looking into the mirror. I saw myself as someone else, a woman with very familiar energy. This woman was my height, broad shoulders, and with the same-colored blonde hair, but a flipped-up style.

The next thing I knew, this woman and I were shaking hands. We were being introduced. Her name was Waylick. My guide shared with me that she was a math teacher and lived around the 1700s. This experience deeply impacted me, because my first love was always to be a math teacher. However, my path led me in another direction and I became a registered nurse.

It was a few years later, I heard that Brian Weiss, a past life regressionist, was going to be holding a workshop in my area. I knew I wanted to attend his session. During the workshop, we did a group past-life regression. The woman I had previously met in my dream state reappeared.

This time I saw that the woman was dying. She was lying in a hospital bed surrounded by her children. I noticed light streaming through the windows and I sensed her time to pass was near. Following the completion of the workshop, my curiosity got the best of me to know if this woman truly existed. Indeed, the Waylick family did exist around that time.

This experience in dream state took place in my actual womb. It was significant, because I was this woman. I was her on another timeline and it was as if I was birthing awareness that I was that math teacher.

> I'm great~full to my spirit guide for introducing me to this part of myself. It explains my connection to the love for math and to the love for teaching.

CHAPTER 11

## St. Joseph

It's the first weekend of my separation from my children's father. My kids and I are on our way to visit my parents at the Cape. We had all been through a lot with the separation, so we were happy to be going to the Cape for rest and relaxation.

We were a few miles from the Bourne Bridge, when I heard a loud bang. It sounded like an explosion. What was that? I thought it might be my tire, so I quickly and safely made it across the highway to the side of the road. I told the kids to carefully get out of the car on the right side and to hike up onto the embankment.

When I got out and checked to see what had happened, sure enough, my right back tire was blown. I had never changed a tire before, so I was a wreck inside at the thought of doing this.

I've been through so much and now this? I know I was fortunate, it could have been much worse. I called my brother and it turned out he was only twenty minutes away, so he could help us.

Shortly after getting off the phone with him, an old wood-paneled station wagon pulled over. I was afraid that this stranger might not have good intentions and I was worried about my children. However, a man in his sixties with a reddish beard and a slight build got out of his car and asked if we needed help.

## THIS IS A VERY IMPORTANT LIFETIME FOR YOU

I said that we were okay and pretended to be on the phone with my brother. The man asked, "Do you want me to take a look at the tire?"

I repeated to him that we were OK. I also told him that my brother was close by and was on his way. I had already taken the spare tire out for my brother to put on.

This man proceeded to tell me that he was a carpenter from the town where I lived. He went on to say that his wife, Mary, was a nurse. I was thinking this is quite a coincidence since he's from the same town as us and his wife is a nurse like I am.

Before I realized it, he had been making conversation while taking off the old tire and putting on the spare. The conversation was so calming, it put me at ease. His energy was very gentle.

I noticed that my brother was now across from us on the highway. He was taking the next exit to come closer. Then I realized the man had completed the task of putting the tire on my car, so I thanked him and offered to pay. However, he said that it was his pleasure and he didn't want compensation.

I asked him his name before he got into his car. He smiled and replied, "Joseph."

Suddenly, I saw my brother's truck was pulling up behind us. I turned my head for just a few seconds, but when I turned back, the man and his car were nowhere to be found. Gone, just like that.

After my brother checked the tire, we all got back into the car, as he said it looked good. We followed him and arrived safely at our parent's house.

I called a friend to share what had happened while driving to my parent's house. My friend is very intuitive. Before I could even explain about this man named Joseph who had stopped to help us, she told me that she had seen a cross in the air above our car. Then I told her about Joseph and she said this was a divine intervention. I agreed with her and told her I felt blessed and protected.

I've always felt a close connection to St. Joseph. Somehow, I knew in this tire blowout experience that something mystical was happening. I was beside myself when this happened on the highway but the whole time, this man, Joseph, was trying to put me at ease, talking to me.

Joseph's occupation was a carpenter and his wife's name was Mary. She was a nurse like I am. He showed up in his old wood-paneled station wagon to help us out of the blue. He stayed with us the whole time, even though I repeatedly assured him that my brother was coming. Then as I turned my head to look at my brother's truck, Joseph mysteriously disappeared and was gone without a trace.

> I knew something miraculous had happened that day.

## CHAPTER 12

## *Fairies*

It was the first weekend that my kids were going to their father's house. We had just separated and were now living in different places. The kids and I were staying with my sister during the selling of our family home. We had only been there a few days.

It was a sad and difficult time for all of us. The kids were going to be with their father this weekend for the first time since our separation.

To comfort myself, I decided to sleep in my daughter's room. I wanted the feeling of her close by. It was on the upper level and one wall was decorated with a huge tree mural. The painted mural had a swing hanging down from one of its branches with painted flowers and butterflies all around it. It was very whimsical and peaceful.

Feeling emotionally exhausted and sad with my kids not being there, I just wanted to go to bed, pull the covers up over my head, and hide from the world. I ended up falling into a deep sleep, only to wake up just as the sun was rising.

I woke up to two pure white fairies, dressed in white flowing dresses. They were dancing around the spindle of the bedpost on the right side near the foot of the bed. They were beautiful, emanating light as they were spiraling, performing pirouettes.

I looked on in amazement, as they were very graceful. Then I blinked and they were gone.

I knew the fairies were there to uplift us all. I am happy and great~full that they appeared to reassure me that we are being watched over.

## CHAPTER 13

# Ye Little Faith

Going through a divorce can be very challenging, especially when children are involved. It's an intricate balancing act. As a parent, you want your children to be emotionally stable through such a difficult time in their lives. In our case, our children had two parents who loved them very much.

In light of this, I worked extremely hard to protect my children from hearing anything negative about their father, as best I could. I tended to shelter them from some of the personal issues we had gone through.

However, as the divorce proceeding dragged on for over two years, it had become very draining. My children and I didn't feel it was ever going to end. I just wanted it to be over.

I was emotionally drained and physically tired, working full-time, taking care of my children, and going through the divorce. It was one of those days when I was feeling sad, defeated, and alone in the house. I prayed to the angels for help and hope.

It was at that moment; I heard a voice. I knew exactly who it was—Yeshua. To me his name is Yeshua, but to many, they know him as Jesus.

I heard a loud voice say three little words, "YE LITTLE FAITH." Then I felt love and peace wash over me.

I thought to myself, *Yes, Yeshua, you are right. I have been doubting my faith, but not anymore.*

I do have faith. I have faith in God, Yeshua, Mary, Angels, justice, and most of all, in myself. That's it. I am done worrying. I needed to go on with my life.

Shortly after this, the proceedings flowed, and we finalized our divorce. We could move on in peace, as best we could.

> I am so great~full for those three little words. My prayers were answered.

# CHAPTER 14

# Smells and Visions

From a young age there was a familiar smell that accompanied a recurring vision. This smell and vision went on for years, but I was perplexed about where this originated from.

In my vision I kept seeing a cream-colored leather back seat of a vintage car. The putrid smell was constant and I knew by the smell and vision that someone had been murdered in this car. This is all I knew—I just didn't know what happened.

Fast forward it was to one day when I had a healing session with my Reiki healer. When she asked me my intention for the session, I shared with her that I was very unhappy with my job and wanted to leave. I had felt this way for a while, but something was holding me there. However, I wasn't sure what it was.

Deep down, I was attached to my students. I was a school nurse for students with special needs. I knew it was because of the administration that I no longer wanted to be there—it was a toxic environment.

After sharing my intent for my Reiki session, she shared a vision of me being a special needs child in a lifetime, where I was wheelchair-bound. In that time period, they institutionalize such a child or eliminate them.

I was quite surprised to hear what she said next. She saw something that took place in the back seat of a car where a child was murdered—I was that child. It was at that exact moment, the putrid smell was gone.

Once the connection of my recurring vision and smell was made, I no longer noticed the putrid smell. My visual memory is clear of this back seat of the car.

> The awareness of what had happened in that life was the information I needed for my healing.

# CHAPTER 15

## AMMA

This took place in Sedona, Arizona, my favorite place in the whole world—my home of homes and a place of mysticism and magic. I am always so happy in Sedona. My friend and I had just arrived. I had talked so much about Sedona that she wanted to experience the energy for herself.

By afternoon, the temperature was too hot to continue meditating out in the red rock, so we decided instead to go shopping at a wonderful metaphysical store. All morning, I kept getting messages of Divine Mother.

As we entered the store, a flyer posted on the wall outside the entrance jumped out at me: AMMA! She is known as the hugging saint from India and was scheduled to be in town this week. She was giving blessings here in Sedona tomorrow. Awesome, this is a sign!

We got up early to catch the sunrise and then went for coffee, before heading to see AMMA at the Sedona Creative Life Center. Upon arriving, we were handed slips of paper with numbers on them, but our numbers were in the hundreds.

When we finally made our way to the door, a tall woman dressed in all white said they were at full capacity. She told us we could come back at 11:00 am for her last offering. What? We couldn't come back at eleven o'clock. We had already committed to taking part in a healing circle that began at eleven. This was our only chance to see her.

She explained, "I'm sorry, it's a fire code." She proceeded to say that we could look around in the gift shop. I couldn't believe it. How could I be so off? I stood there with my friend, my eyes filling with tears. I knew I was going to cry. I needed air and I needed to clear my head. My intuition was telling me one thing, while this woman was telling me another.

My friend said she was going to look around in the gift shop before we left, so I went outside and sat on one of the benches. Tears poured down my face. That's one thing about Sedona—when you're in this energy, all the emotions are amplified one hundred-fold.

I couldn't believe it. I don't understand the Universe. All the messages I have been receiving since we landed in Sedona were "Divine Mother."

That morning in meditation, a great turtle presented herself, which means Mother Earth. As we walked to the overlook at Sky Ranch Lodge to participate in chi gong, a mother road runner and her little chicks ran across the road in front of us. The flyer I saw at the store could have been in neon lights for all I know. It jumped out at me saying AMMA.

We get here and can't get in! I just couldn't understand it—I couldn't process it, so I felt like giving up. I must be totally off with my guidance. All signs pointed to the mother connection.

As I sat in the garden waiting for my friend, I prayed for help. I also prayed with the intent to converse with AMMA. I asked her why I was so misguided. I prayed that if she was here, would she please come out and get us.

I was so overwhelmed with emotion. it was much like the time I saw Sai Ma. I felt the sun on my face, the energy flowing up thru my body, and a gentle breeze caressed my cheek, so I prayed.

I don't know how long I had been sitting there praying, when my friend came running out, loudly calling my name.

"What—what's the matter?" I ask.

She proceeds to tell me with boasting energy that the woman from the door came up to her in the gift shop. Admittedly said she wasn't sure why she was saying this, but that AMMA wasn't here yet. "So if you want to go and get your friend, you both can come with us to greet AMMA at the car."

I found out later the custom is to greet AMMA at the chauffeured car with flowers and walk her into the building. The woman said we could go with them to greet the Divine Mother, if we would like.

I was very excited, so I said, "Oh, yes!"

The woman in white looked straight at me, smiled, and nodded as a gesture to follow her down the path to the circular drive, so we followed.

One woman carried a beautifully decorated umbrella, draped in bright fresh flowers all over the top, and descending the sides in oranges, pinks, and yellows—it was breathtaking.

As AMMA gracefully stepped out of the car, a woman gently covered her head with the umbrella of flowers. AMMA turned to both of us, bowed her head and blessed us. *Oh my God! She knew. She heard and answered my prayers.*

The feeling of PURE LOVE enveloped me—it filled the air. No separation, just complete unity. It was amazing! Better than I could ever imagine. Undoubtedly, it was better than being inside the building to witness her presence.

It was perfect divination. All is in Divine Order—I forget this at times. As I write this, I am reminded!

**Thank you, Divine Mother!**

That wasn't my only interaction with AMMA. I have had the honor of meeting with her two other times. I didn't think it was going to be possible to see her this time either. AMMA was scheduled to be here in Massachusetts during a busy time of the year. The dates of her event coincided with a wedding shower I had already committed to attend.

However, this was the only time AMMA was offering darshan in this area. Darshan is a blessing given by a holy person, a deity in this case, the Blessed Mother of India. I was truly disappointed that I couldn't go. There was no way I could change things—at least I didn't think so. Therefore, I had to accept it.

The day before the shower, I was driving on the highway, when a truck cut me off. The writing on the truck spelled, AMMA. What the heck? What's the Universe trying to do? Rub it in, that I can't go?

I didn't think the Universe operated this way. I thought it was a human thing to focus on the downside of things. I couldn't figure it out. Why would I see this truck with AMMA on it?

I arrived home still disappointed and checked my messages. The shower luncheon had been cancelled.

---

Oh, Universe, you are amazing!
Needless to say, I saw AMMA. It was an honor to get a hug and a blessing from this loving Hugging Saint.

---

CHAPTER 16

# Divinely Orchestrated

Ever have one of those days that you feel everything falls on your shoulders? This was one of those days. I was in the middle of doing something. but our dog needed to go out. After asking several times if someone could take the dog out, it seemed everyone was too busy.

As a parent, never mind being a single parent, that happens a lot. My frustration got to me, but our dog needed to go out, so I got his leash and took him out the front door.

I won't deny it—I was very frustrated. You hope when you ask your kids to do something that they will and not make you ask repeatedly. This time, it wasn't worth it, as our dog was the one that had to suffer.

As I was walking down the brick stairs, I somehow got tangled up in the leash and tripped and fell on my face, mainly hitting the right side of my forehead, brow, and upper cheek. I had a huge abrasion, was bleeding, and immediately bruised.

My face and head hurt like hell. I should have gone to the hospital, as I probably had a concussion. However, I had an appointment I didn't want to miss with Max, the Crystal Skull. I had made this appointment a month in advance.

I gently washed my face, bandaged it as best I could, grabbed a bag of ice, and jumped into the car. The metaphysical store was about twenty minutes away.

Once I arrived, one of the staff looked at me with a stunned face. I could only imagine what he was thinking. Something like, "Aren't you in the wrong place? The hospital is down the street."

When it was my turn to see Max, I was intuitively guided to put my forehead right up to his. He was communicating with me, assuring me he could heal my face. I immediately felt the energy and instantly began feeling better.

Wow, who would ever have thought? It felt as if the appointment I had made a month earlier was for a healing. Little did I know my healing would be emotional *and* physical.

---

Everything is in Divine Order.
Max came through and I am
forever great-full.

---

Things like this seem to happen in my life. A similar situation happened prior to my dad's transition to Spirit. I had made an appointment with Stewart Pearce for a reading and the first availability was a month away in March. In addition to the reading, he included an audio recording of angelic chanting.

My dad passed away within a day of my arrival in March. Later that day, when filled with emotion, I realized I had the reading with Stewart Pearce. I was able to ease my grief with the angelic chant recording I had been sent.

I shared with Stewart that my dad had passed earlier that morning. He confirmed that the timing of this reading was divinely orchestrated. He shared that one of my life's purposes was to help others transition to Spirit with a sense of peace, grace, and love.

I know that I helped with my beloved dad's passing. Spirit guides me frequently and this was an example of that.

Thank you to the Divine
for this experience.

## CHAPTER 17

# My Native American Chief

My business partner and I were looking for a space for our wellness center in Massachusetts. This accomplishment was heavy on my mind as I went to sleep that night. Later that night, I had a dream that was centered around a stone house.

Could this be our wellness center? The house was located on lush greenery with lots of shade trees around it. A long driveway allowed you to drive up past a prominent stone wall. Beyond the wall, I saw a yellow meadow, so I decided to get out and sit on it.

From the top of the wall was a steep drop to the meadow below. While looking out to the furthest part of the meadow, I noticed a huge ostrich with green and yellow feathers. As I looked at the bird, it caught me staring and began running towards me flapping its wings. At first, I didn't realize how enormous it was!

As it approached, it flew up to meet me on the stone wall. Suddenly, the ostrich transformed into the face of my Native American chief. His thin, gray hair was long and outlined his face. He had a serious face, though I felt the unconditional love emanating from him.

The green and yellow feathers transformed into his headdress. My Native American guide's ostrich transformation continued. His back turned into a red canoe. He flew up to greet me and invited me to join him in the canoe, so I did. We flew off together in the red canoe.

My chief told me his name was Star Maker. He revealed that in a past or concurrent life, I was a medicine woman in the Blackfoot Tribe with him. My name was Crystal Water Medicine Woman.

Star Maker was showing me other options for my future work. He went on to reveal to me that I was to learn from this wellness center and from the partner relationship. This was essential so that I could move forward with my work when it was time.

> He said, "You're going to be doing this work here for now. However, this is just the beginning. There is much more to come, Crystal Water Medicine Woman."

## CHAPTER 18

# Kwan Yin

I was starting a new business with a new partner. We were in the process of looking for a space for our wellness center. We had temporarily moved it into the basement of my house.

The energy in my home is amazing. Whenever my business partner and I meditated in this space, it was more like channeling. We would often get information directly from Spirit.

One day in our meditation we received information that wherever this wellness center would be located, Kwan Yin would be a part of it. In another meditation, we received the message that Kwan Yin will be present guiding us and she will be facing the altar we create in this new space. Kwan Yin is known as the Buddhist Goddess of compassion. These channeled messages were very important, so we began to write them down.

It was summer, when we finally found our new wellness center. However, the space wasn't exactly in a location you would think was where a wellness center would be located. This wasn't a serene, wooded area, but instead it was in an old building next to the train station.

We were drawn to it primarily because of the energy we felt in it. Our landlord was great and welcomed the idea of a wellness center in this space. The only thing needed was a new coat of paint.

We finished painting and brought in the furniture. We didn't need much—a few tables, folding chairs, and massage tables. We decided on where our altar would be and made it one of the meditation areas.

While sitting blessing our new space, Kwan Yin appeared to me. A four-foot, side portrait of Kwan Yin facing our altar appeared in the stucco. She's stunningly beautiful and caught my breath.

I had forgotten about the channeling initially, until it sunk in. She's here. This is a sign. Everyone who came into our center could see Kwan Yin in the stucco wall.

To our surprise, Kwan Yin wasn't the only presence here. In one of the corners of the room, Ganesh appeared on the stucco wall. Ganesh is my beloved elephant-headed friend who frequently appeared in my childhood dreams. Many who came to the wellness center saw other deities.

We received another surprise in our space when my friend came in and saw Jesus in the upper left-hand corner of the room. There was a painting of him in the corner, the Prince of Peace, which I thought she was talking about. But that wasn't what she saw.

She pointed up higher than the painting. This is where she saw Jesus, up in the corner stucco, where he appeared to be watching over us wearing what seemed like a wreath of thorns on his head. This was a sacred space where we felt truly blessed.

I wonder if people would believe it, if they hadn't seen it themselves. However, they did see it and they were all witnesses to what beautiful energy this wellness center held. Kwan Yin, Ganesh, and Jesus were always present and visible to all in this space.

When I did healings or meditations in this space, these Divine beings were always present. I am great-full.

# CHAPTER 19

# Sedona Healing Magic

Here I am sitting in my favorite spot at Cathedral Rock in Sedona, Arizona. It was a long trip, getting here. It's 1:00 a.m. and my hotel room number is 222. What 222 means to me is "have faith, pay attention to synchronicities, and loving relationships." It's a sign that something important is about to take place.

Before I left for my trip, I had a healing session. I was vibrating from head to toe, and crying throughout the session. I was immersed in unconditional love. It was amazing. I could feel the Love from God pulsating through me, knowing it was for me to experience and to share. It's difficult to describe—you just weep.

As I am writing this, a lady bug is crawling on me. The lady bug symbolizes a deep Love, kindness, and compassion for self and others. I know it's coming together with all these signs presenting themselves. I must be patient. It's all happening in Divine timing and I am so great~full.

I felt it was time to share my favorite spot.

> As I sit near the creek, I decided to put my crystals in the water to cleanse.

I saw some people trying to take a picture with Cathedral Rock in the background. I told them I was leaving and they could take my spot for their picture. Then I asked if they wanted me to take a picture of them. Excitedly they said yes and were great~full.

They shared that they were a family. They came here together to Sedona because their dad had died over the summer and they wanted to celebrate his life here. I immediately felt their father's presence, so I told them. I had goosebumps from head to toe and so did they—confirmation. They were elated, saying I was a conduit for this to happen. We all knew it at the time—this was no coincidence.

The two sisters were nurses. One of them was named Nancy. The other two worked in schools. We discovered that we had so much in common and that this was not a coincidence. I'm a nurse and I work in a school. We all felt I was brought there to be with them on this occasion.

They continued walking on the path along the creek, so I decided to stay here and meditate—this place has such beautiful energy. I am so great~full.

While I meditated, I received a message that told me that if I ever crossed paths with them again, I needed to give each one a crystal stone. Suddenly, I turned around and saw them sitting together with their backs towards me. It was such a beautiful scene that I took a picture and went over to share it with them.

We were all standing together in a circle talking, when something happened. I felt the strong presence of a boy who had passed over and I heard the name started with the letter J.

I wondered why I was getting this message and if it might be related to this group. When I asked them if they knew a John or Jonathan, the person named Chuck, his eyes filled with tears and he couldn't contain himself. Then, the rest of the family started to cry, too.

# THIS IS A VERY IMPORTANT LIFETIME FOR YOU

Chuck gasped and said that this was his son Jonathan, who had died from an asthma attack at twelve years of age. Chuck proceeded to share his feelings of guilt, as he blamed himself for his death. Jonathan told me that his dad needed to let go of the guilt, as it wasn't his fault.

Jonathan went on to say that he would send a butterfly from the other side to let his father know that he's OK. Within a few seconds, a beautiful yellow butterfly landed on Chuck's hand. We all screamed. This was the sign that Jonathan had promised to send to let his father know that he's OK.

What I didn't realize was that one of Chuck's sisters had prayed for a black and yellow striped butterfly to come to Chuck as a sign from Jonathan. This had just happened prior to us meeting. Here was a double confirmation from Jonathan that he's OK.

We all began talking about spirit, contracts in this lifetime, and forgiveness. I said I brought some crystal stones and that I wished to give them each a stone. They were stunned and told me that they had made a pact when they were at the airport. The agreement was that they would each go home with a stone from Sedona honoring their late father and reminding them of him.

They couldn't believe I was offering this gift to them. They said I was sent by Jonathan and their father to give them what they had prayed for. They believed that this was heavenly orchestrated.

Now I understand that the healing I received prior to coming to Sedona was for me to receive and share. It was a gift from God for a healing for this grieving family. Jonathan and his grandfather were a big part of this family's healing journey. I felt blessed to be a conduit for this blessed gift.

When I got back to my hotel room, I called my friend. As I was telling her about what happened at Cathedral Rock with this family, a yellow butterfly flew by my window. This was the third confirmation from Jonathan of everything that had happened.

Thank you, Jonathan. Later that day, as I was driving to the chapel of the Holy Cross, I understood that Jonathan was the one who sent me to his family. Jonathan somehow knew I worked as a school nurse and with kids who had asthma.

That night I had a dream that I needed to use an EpiPen for a boy having an allergic reaction. In my dream, the boy appeared to have a very swollen face. I wondered if that's how fast it had happened for Jonathan. I knew in my heart this was Jonathan's way of showing me how he died. It happened so quickly that no one could have done anything to save him.

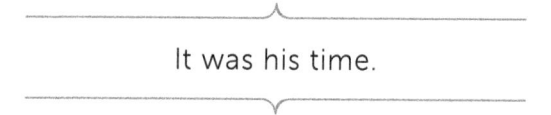

It was his time.

It's been many years since I first met Jonathan's family in Sedona. I am still in touch with Chuck and his siblings, and he and I correspond a couple of times a year. Jonathan also continues to come to me every now and then.

A few years ago, on Father's Day, Jonathan wanted me to let his dad know how much he loves him and continued to encourage Chuck to let go of his guilt surrounding his passing.

To my surprise, Jonathan also revealed that my daughter, Kelsey, who transitioned as an infant and Jonathan were working together to help children cross over to the other side. Chuck confirmed this information when he told me that Jonathan's mother had a dream where Jonathan was helping another child cross over.

Chuck is always very appreciative when I give him messages. It's beautiful and comforting to receive signs and messages from Spirit.

## CHAPTER 20

# A Gift from Great Spirit

It's my birthday, but it started out just like most other days, until I received a gift from Great Spirit in dreamtime. My dream begins as I am standing looking at my childhood home. I'm at the entrance to the kitchen. I am drawn to the big picture window there, which has a huge white shade that is drawn down and closed. I am guided to walk over and pull the shade up to see what is outside.

To my amazement, the pool and fence that would've been there are missing from the backyard. Instead, there's a huge pond and I can see our neighborhood church, Saint Timothy's. It is the church our family attended on Sundays and holidays.

Then this scene transformed into a Thomas Kinkaid painting with a beautiful village surrounding the church on the furthest side of the pond with a grassy knoll about 20 feet from the pond.

To my astonishment, a huge white unicorn slowly enters the pond and canters through the water to the other side. It is pure white and as big as a Clydesdale horse. Two other unicorns follow behind this one. Overwhelming peace pours over me as I observe these magnificent animals make their way through the water.

I blink and suddenly I am now outside, standing on the grassy knoll. I can smell the fresh air and feel the wind on my face. Oh, what's happening? I sense the ground rumbling under my feet.

It feels and sounds like a stampede of horses. Horses are running by me, as if they don't see me as they rush towards the pond.

I see Native American Indian men riding bareback on horses. These men are slender and fit, with feathers and beads dangling from their long black hair. They are riding beautiful pintos, white horses with light brown markings and have spears in their hands.

I see a Native American man who, if provoked, is ready to throw his spear. The group is moving very quickly through the water toward the middle of the pond. I feared it was the unicorns they were hunting. Thankfully, the unicorns had already passed by, as I can no longer see them, so they are safe.

Then I notice an inlet of land on the upper side of the pond, where some white buffalo are grazing. I thought to myself, *I hope they aren't hunting the buffalo.* White buffalo are sacred and rare and considered peace bearers for humanity. Intuitively, I realize the Native American men were there to protect the white buffalo from harm's way.

This was truly a gift to have this experience. When I awoke, I realized I was one of the Native Americans riding bareback on my horse, helping to protect the unicorns and the sacred white buffalo. This dream awakened my senses and was as real as if I were wide awake. I knew I had witnessed a lifetime as a Native American man in dreamtime.

## CHAPTER 21

# Durga~Divine Mother

It was summer and my business partner and I were opening our healing center. We were preparing for our first event, "Tea and Chi." I am on my way to the store to buy a tablecloth for the opening, but the event requires conservative purchasing.

I am in the home section of the store when I notice a beautiful glass statue of a Hindu goddess. She has several arms raised around her head, as if she is the center of a flower, and her arms are the petals. I am not sure if this is Lakshmi, but she is beautiful. I want her for our center, but the price tag is telling me something different, so she must be for another time.

However, I am being drawn to her once again on my way to the tablecloths. I decided to pick her up and hold her. Immediately I felt a strange sensation inside my heart, but I still knew I had to get the tablecloth.

Sadly, I placed her back down. Then, I thought to myself *How can I get both?* I knew that I came for the tablecloth, so I had to get it. Suddenly, I could hear the goddess talking to me. I picked her up again, but this time, I walked directly to Checkout.

When I returned to our wellness center, my partner asked where the tablecloth was. I said that I had found something even better and showed him the statue of the goddess. The one great thing about him is that he gets it. When I handed him the goddess, he immediately took her and created a sacred space on our altar for her. We both knew she was home. Her energy is amazing.

Shortly after, we sat on the floor in meditation in a state of gratitude with this beautiful goddess with the many arms. I could sense her energy as we sat in silence, as it was palpable as it moved throughout my body and surrounded me.

As we came back from meditation to our surroundings, my partner shared with me something extraordinary. He said there was a pure stream of white light flowing down onto the top of my head during our meditation. It appeared as if she was becoming one with my energy. He was confirming what I was experiencing. Tears rolled down my face. I felt a deep feeling of unconditional love exuding throughout my being.

People really enjoyed the "Tea and Chi" event at our healing center that evening. I drove home, both exhilarated and exhausted. I fell asleep right away and was sleeping peacefully when I was awakened by a soothing voice speaking to me.

It was the same voice I had heard while shopping for the tablecloth. I saw an arm coming down from my bedroom ceiling. This wasn't a dream—I was awake with my eyes wide open. I was seeing this clearly, knowing there was nothing to fear. I felt pure divine love and peace. A female voice was speaking to me telepathically, telling me to pay attention to this hand position.

I realized that the skin color was of Indian descent. The hand was positioned with the index and middle finger extended as if pointing down. At the same time, the ring and pinky fingers were bent down at the knuckles. The thumb was pressing on the side of the bent ring finger. It's clear to me that this hand position was important. The hand is now holding my hand. The peace and love I felt was incredible. I closed my eyes for a second and the arm was gone. I wondered why this was happening.

I looked out my bedroom window to see a huge blue face in the tree outside. The face filled the top half of a large pine tree. A voice spoke and said, "I am Durga, the Divine Mother."

Later that day in meditation, I asked for guidance on what to do with this experience and the hand position. I was told I would know in time. I looked up online hand positions and discovered they are called mudras. Jesus, Buddha, and Hindu Gods and Goddesses are seen using them, in many forms. The mudra presented to me was different from those I had researched and found online. I asked a few healer friends about this mudra that was shown to me by the goddess. They consistently replied that they had never seen this mudra before.

Two years later, I am at one of my healer friend's homes and she starts using the exact mudra that I was shown. When I asked her about the mudra she was using, she explained that she learned it while on a healing retreat. She received it from Vywamus, an ascended master. This was the same mudra I received two years ago from Durga.

Another synchronicity with this mudra was when I was introduced to an elderly woman, who was an author and mystic. She showed me some mudras from her book. The woman saw the surprised look on my face as she turned the page and asked if something seemed familiar. I told her I recognized the mudra. It was the same one I saw when the hand came down from the ceiling years ago. Her response was, "I know, you and the mudra are one."

I use this mudra in my healing sessions. I trust in the healing presence of the Divine Mother. This was a gift I was given.

The feeling I received while sitting with this woman was as if she had been my teacher before. However, this was impossible, because I had just been introduced to her. I must have known her in a past life. She possessed a wisdom beyond this time and space. She was pointing out to me that this mudra was important for me to discover, so I could use it with my clients in my healing practice.

I wondered if Durga had orchestrated this to assist me in the evolution of my healing practice. I was great~full for the synchronicities and continue to use this to this day in my healing sessions with clients.

## CHAPTER 22

## Wolf

Life can be challenging at times, especially with relationships. I had one that ended with a close friend. I was great~full for the friendship, but it had become very negative and wasn't healthy for me. It came to a head when she said she couldn't be friends with me. To be honest, I was relieved, as I was trying to find ways of ending it.

This person was psychic and she continually garnered negative information and would always share it with me. Occasionally is okay, but to hear doom and gloom all the time, I knew something was off with her. Eventually it was like a red flag. My inner voice was telling me that I was lowering my frequency with this kind of information. It was difficult to end our friendship, as I really liked her. She delved into animal totems too and personally identified with the Hawk.

A few days after we parted ways, I was standing in my kitchen and heard a screeching hawk in my backyard. I knew instantly it was her. It gave me chills from head to toe and made me feel like I needed protection.

I called one of my healer friends and shared what was happening. While on the phone, I went out the front door and walked to the side of my house. There I saw a huge hawk in flight. She was flying from one side to the other of my house in the direction towards the backwoods of my neighbors.

To be honest, I felt very unsettled. There are people who use energy in a negative way and I felt the person with whom I had ended my friendship had sent this hawk.

First, I shared my uneasiness with my friend on the phone. Then, I walked back towards the front of the house with my dog on his leash. I knew we needed protection. I commanded out loud to the Universe, "Protect me!" I screamed it out. (My poor dear friend on the phone got an earful.) But I got my answer loud and clear. It was instantaneous and I knew I was protected.

I immediately saw a brown bushy wolf with a full coat of hair appear out of nowhere in broad daylight. As I watched the wolf, he moved deliberately in between my front yard and my neighbor's. He made his way slowly towards my backyard exactly where the hawk was.

I couldn't believe my eyes. I thought, *Oh My God, this wolf could seriously hurt my dog*. But suddenly I shifted into a feeling of absolute calm. I knew we were being protected and that this was Wolf Medicine. I don't know if this was my spirit guide shape-shifting into a wolf for my protection or if this wolf was one of my animal totems. It really didn't matter. I just knew we were loved and protected from any harm.

Thank you, Great Spirit, and<br>thank you, Wolf Medicine.

CHAPTER 23

# Miracle Man

I was asked by one of my best friends to get a booth at a health fair in town, as I would be offering Reiki sessions. My friend was one of my biggest supporters after experiencing a session herself. I love her for that.

As I set up my booth in the gym, an older gentleman, in his late seventies, stopped to ask what I did. I told him I was offering Reiki sessions. He said he was working with the massage therapist at her booth, but would love to try Reiki. He shared that he had been experiencing extreme fatigue and thought this could help. He said he would come back when it wasn't busy.

Later that afternoon, an announcement came across the loudspeaker that a presentation was about to start, so everyone began leaving for it. The older gentleman decided to come back to my booth during the presentation.

He sat in the chair and I placed my hands on his shoulders. Reiki flows instantly when I put my hands on anyone. Immediately he began to violently shake. His body touched my display table, knocking things off. I wasn't quite sure what was happening, as this has never happened before.

I was about to remove my hands from his shoulders when I heard a voice. I knew it was Archangel Michael. He said, "Stay with it. It's okay, stay with it."

I intuitively felt a foreign presence within this man's body. I called in my Spiritual Team and angels to help him. I knew Archangel Michael was protecting me and guiding me throughout the healing.

As I continued doing Reiki, I sensed something was lifting from his body. The shaking stopped instantly. It seemed he had just experienced a huge release.

He turned to me, wondering what had just happened. I didn't want to scare him by sharing what I was receiving.

He said, "Do you know who I am? I've been named the Miracle Man—twice." He shared that he had a cardiac arrest and died twice in the Emergency Room. The medical staff named him the Miracle Man.

I had wondered how this foreign energy that I sensed had entered his body in the first place. Now it made sense—it must have entered his body when he died in the Emergency Room.

The man asked if other clients shook uncontrollably like that during a Reiki session, I said, "Not usually."

He said that he felt so much better and lighter after this session and was surprised by how good he felt. It was interesting, because at the time of his session, the gym was completely empty. Everyone was at the announced presentation, so his session was divinely orchestrated. Spirit helped everyone leave the gym, so that there was less chance of this foreign energy attaching to someone else while being escorted to the light.

As the man was leaving, he thanked me profusely and walked back to his booth. He kept turning back to look at me, as if in disbelief of what he had just experienced.

I knew my spiritual team and I had released a dense energy from this man. If left untouched, it could have resulted in a formidable disease in his body. This was a first for me—to release something of this magnitude.

Since my experience with this man, I've had other Reiki sessions requiring a removal of dense, heavy energy, but nothing that compared to the depth of negative energy this man held in his body.

Thank you, Spiritual Team,
for assisting us.

## CHAPTER 24

# Lucid Dreaming – A Mermaid's Freedom from Bondage

Dreamtime begins with finding myself on the beach standing in front of a mermaid curled up in the fetal position. She was very petite, but her wrists were in shackles and she was chained to the rocks directly behind her. She reminded me of the mermaids that were at the bottom of the ocean being held captive by Ursula in *The Little Mermaid movie*. This little mermaid's eyes were hollow, sunken in, and lifeless.

I am standing with my clipboard in hand by the petite mermaid shackled to the rocks. I'm negotiating terms for her release from the controls of these evil men. This release of terms involves their past karmic bondage patterns and the abuse of mermaids. As the release is secured from these men, you could see her shackles fall to the sand. She has been freed, so now it's time for her to rest.

I turned away to look at another mermaid who has also been freed. She stood six feet tall, with long black hair wrapped on top of her head and decorated with beautiful exotic flowers. This mermaid looked like a Polynesian Goddess.

She was standing on land likely for the last time, before diving back into the water to go home. She exuded heartfelt gratitude and sent it directly to my heart. Tears flowed down my face. For I too in this lifetime have known both feelings of powerlessness and what it felt like to regain my freedom.

I recognized these two mermaids, who are in my present lifetime. One is a close friend, whom I met when I gave her a Reiki session at a medical facility. We are Reiki Masters and intuitives. She was undergoing treatment for breast cancer. She's a tall, beautiful Asian woman, like one of the mermaids in my dream.

In my Reiki sessions with her, we sensed mermaids coming into the session's week after week. The other mermaid I had met on several occasions. She was the future daughter-in-law of my friend, who was undergoing treatment for cancer. She was the shackled mermaid in my dream.

It amazes me how we travel in these soul groups, returning to earth to experience, learn our spiritual lessons, and create. As we release what shackles us, we stand more in our power, setting ourselves free.

# CHAPTER 25

# A Lady in the Elevator

This was a dream. I found myself standing in an old hotel elevator, which had wooden framework inside. There were just the two of us. A very tall, thin woman stood to my right, as we both were facing the door. I didn't see her face, but felt her Presence.

As the doors closed in front of us, I pushed button #1. Suddenly the woman whispered, "Oh, no," and pushed #12, the highest floor option in the elevator. Then I woke up.

I had a trip planned, as my friend and I were excited to be going to New York to see Patricia Cota Robles. We had planned this trip for quite a while. We drove to Westport, Connecticut, parked our car, and took the train into New York City.

Once there, we took a cab from Grand Central Station to the Pennsylvania Hotel on Pennsylvania Avenue, where the event was being held. We arrived early to allow enough time to acquire good seats. I was just so happy to be there.

As we entered the hotel, large groups of people were moving about. Some were arriving like us, while others were leaving. Many seemed to be just hanging out in different areas, as there were several events happening at this hotel.

We immediately tried to find out where Patricia would be speaking. Of course, it was going to be on the 18th floor, the top level. After all, it was all about ascension. I instantly recalled another dream, where there was a neon green sign shaped like a huge arrow that said, ASCENSION THIS WAY. It was pointing to the right.

They had ten elevators, five on either side. We finally made it to the top in one of those old rattling elevators—I just wanted to get up there quickly. When we finally exited the elevator on the 18th floor, we proceeded to look for more information posted about where our event was being held.

Straight across from us was a woman with a beautiful smile, who was greeting people. She was instructing everyone to proceed down the hallway to the right and into the ballroom, where the event was being held.

As we entered, many attendees were already seated. It appeared that the first six rows were already taken. My friend said she wanted to go to the bathroom first, but I shared that we might want to grab our chairs before they were taken. She agreed.

As we walked up to about the seventh row, which had open chairs, we started to place our stuff into two empty seats. However, I intuitively received a message to look at the first few rows, a message I immediately trusted, so I proceeded to the first row.

There were two empty chairs, so I asked a woman across the way if she knew if these were available. She said that if there wasn't anything on the chairs, then they were ours—great!

I was very drawn to a beautiful scarf draped on the chair next to the open two chairs. I quickly put my stuff down on one and my friend dropped hers on the other. Then we were off to the bathroom.

As we were coming back from the bathroom, there stood Patricia in the hallway. She was dressed in a beautiful light blue suit, and looked very well put together.

My friend said, "This is a great sign—it's good luck." Then we settled into our seats. I was sitting next to the chair with the beautiful scarf. I closed my eyes to meditate before the event started.

When I opened my eyes, I couldn't believe it! Patricia was sitting next to me. *Oh, wow,* I thought to myself, *I had better clear my energy. She's going to notice some negativity.*

It was surreal. My friend elbowed me. People were coming up to Patricia and talking with her. I felt badly. She was sitting with her hands in a mudra, probably trying to meditate before she was to present from the podium.

I didn't want to bother her, but then again, I didn't want to be rude and not say anything. So I turned to her, with my heart filled with love and sincerity and said, "Thank You!"

In return, she said, "You're welcome." The tears ran down my face. Here is the woman who has brought forth the Violet Flame to Humanity. For the past five years, I've been running a Violet Flame Weekly Meditation Group—all because of her. WOW!

I then closed my eyes and felt Divine presence within me. Moments later, I opened my eyes to see Patricia now standing on the podium. *How did she get up there without me noticing her leave her seat?* I guess I'm not really surprised—she's ascended.

It wasn't until right before falling asleep that night that I recalled my dream of the woman in the old elevator. It was her—Patricia Cota Robles! She was reminding me to choose the highest floor. Along with the dream of the neon green arrow leading to ascension, it looked like the top floor plan for her event. Both messages were of ascension. We truly are being guided.

Our dreams are just one of the many ways we receive guidance. Our dreams can show us events before they happen. This was a great example of that.

# CHAPTER 26

# *Ixchel*

I was traveling to Mexico with two of my best friends from junior high school and another friend who had joined us. We were on our way to celebrate our 50th birthdays together. We had made a decision a long time ago that when we turned 50, we would celebrate our birthdays by going somewhere special together. This birthday vacation would be fun, lying in the sun, and just relaxing. I was hoping for a spiritual experience, too, which would be the icing on the cake for me.

When the time came, we decided on an all-inclusive trip to the Mayan Riviera. I was hesitant at first—primarily because of the human sacrifices that were performed in this area over thousands of years. I felt that I had lived a few lifetimes there and that in one of those lifetimes, I was sacrificed. This is what held me back previously from going there until now. Something had shifted and Spirit wanted me to go there—it was time.

We booked our trip six months in advance. Shortly after booking it, I started to research known spiritual places associated with the region. I knew some ruins were there and somehow felt that this is where I needed to go.

I talked about visiting some ruins with my friends, but they weren't interested. However, I didn't want to go alone. I felt that someone needed to go with me. Finally, one of my friends agreed to accompany me, if it was safe. Of course, it would be safe. I couldn't imagine what she was talking about, yet little did I know what was about to happen.

It had been about a year since I started a weekly meditation group, specifically working with the Violet Flame, an amazing tool that Spirit provided to me. St. Germaine specifically helps transmute negative energy.

Working with the Violet Flame is a way to raise our vibration and consciousness to a higher level for ourselves and for all of humanity. The home of the Mayans would be a good place to use the tool of the Violet Flame. What better place to use this than one that was consumed with years of torture and abuse to so many. On the flipside, the Mayans did have many wonderful medicine women, men, and Shamans, who also healed people.

Once we arrived at the airport, we needed to look for our driver. Before leaving we were told to make sure we were getting into the right van, one that would take us directly to our hotel to avoid scams. We were staying at a Princess hotel and champagne awaited us as we walked into the hotel. This is a fun reminder to treat ourselves like princesses for the week.

Before I continue with this story, I want to share some important information that happened before we left on our trip, when I was working at my school. This knowledge will bring this whole Mayan experience full circle in the end.

A co-worker from school was going on a church trip with her mother to Lourdes. I had given her two rose quartz crystals to offer for Mother Mary at Lourdes. I didn't want to put a lot of pressure on my co-worker, in case she forgot. I told her if she was able to do this, I would be great-full. I wanted to honor Mother Mary for always being with me. I would like to make a separate trip in the future, as it's high on my bucket list.

Now, back to my Mayan experience. We arrived at our Princess hotel, which was so very beautiful. We checked in, changed our clothes, and decided to stroll down to the ocean. There, we met Charlie, our very sweet Cabana boy for the week. We tipped him well, knowing that he was saving for college. Our group had such fun together, including enjoying time with our Cabana boy, so I knew we were in for a crazy week.

Upon returning from the beach, my friend and I checked in with the front desk to set up a day excursion. After doing some research, we picked Tulum, as a trip was scheduled to go there on Tuesday. This would give us a few days to enjoy the beach and then go to Tulum before our flight home.

Monday night, we had dinner at a Japanese restaurant that served sushi. I don't usually eat sushi, but I thought a vegetarian California roll sounded good.

I guessed wrong, because I was violently ill all night. I was so worried that I might not be well enough to take the trip to Tulum. I was thinking, *How can I take a catamaran trip on the water feeling this way?*

Sure enough, when I awoke the next morning, I was still ill and couldn't travel. My friend was kind enough to go to the tour table in the lobby and change the date of our Catamaran trip. Although she tried to reschedule it for the next day, the only day the boat sailed was Thursday. However, by Wednesday, I was already feeling better, so we went to relax on lounge chairs on the beach. We had scheduled massage appointments for later that day, as I was recuperating, so we were once again relaxing and having a good time.

While lying on the lounge chairs, facing the gorgeous ocean, I noticed a woman coming in our direction with jewelry hanging off her arm. I remembered that when checking in to the hotel, we were told not to buy anything from anyone who comes up to us on the beach—especially we should not buy any jewelry from them. To ignore her, I decided to just close my eyes and continue listening to my iPod. I also called in my guides, angels, Yeshua, and Mother Mary.

Shortly afterwards, my friend said to us, "Did you see that?"

I responded, "No, what?"

She said, "The woman selling the jewelry walked up to the base of our chairs. When she approached my chair, she blessed herself three times." I thought to myself, *Is that a good sign or not?*

I was so excited when Thursday morning finally arrived. First we walked down to where all the tours were supposed to meet. Then we waited and waited in the hot sun. We watched people board their tour buses and off they went. That is, everyone was gone, except us.

Did we miss our transportation? Something was wrong here. I started feeling anxious. I came here to go on this trip, so I had to go there. Tulum was calling me, as I could feel a strong energetic pull to go there.

We began asking the few people who were left about the transportation for the Catamaran trip. No one had even heard of a Catamaran trip to Tulum. Someone asked, "How would you board a Catamaran, since there's no nearby dock?"

Are you kidding me? I was getting upset, as I didn't understand why this was happening. Tulum was an important place to visit and I must go there. Surely Spirit wouldn't have me come all this way and then lead me on a wild goose chase.

My friend decided to call the hotel front desk to talk to Damian, since we had booked the trip through him. I remembered thinking, *This is getting weird—his name is Damian?*

The hotel clerk said the trip was canceled. He couldn't refund us the money today, but he could if, we came back tomorrow. At that point, I didn't care about the $90.00 we each paid. I was upset about the trip being cancelled. This meant I wasn't going to Tulum. How could this happen?

The person at the travel company said we could take a cab to Tulum. However, one of my friends said she didn't feel that it was safe to take a cab. Now my anxiety was really escalating.

Then the owner of the travel company offered to hire a private car to drive us, but no tour. He assured us it would be safe traveling with a private driver. The cost was the same minus the tour through the ruins.

This was a definite YES! I quickly paid and waited outside on the bench for our ride. A white, beat-up Volkswagen bus pulled up. We were told, "This is him."

My friend looked at me in desperation with fear in her eyes. I reassured her that we would be okay. The man from the Tourist Company said that the driver spoke a little English—okay, some English is good. He further informed us that he knew we were going to Tulum.

We stepped up and climbed into the back seat of the van. As we got settled, the driver turned around and in broken English, said, "Hi, my name is Angel."

*Thank you, GOD,* I thought to myself. Hearing that his name was Angel, I knew we would be fine. *This is a sign.* As we drove, my breathing slowly started to become labored. I felt a heaviness on my chest and my anxiety returned.

*What's going on?* That's when I began putting it all together. There was the jewelry woman on the beach blessing herself with the sign of the cross and standing at my feet, Damian sold us a catamaran trip that didn't exist and we never saw Damian again, I became deathly ill from sushi and something or someone is trying to block us from going to Tulum.

It seems there might be some negative forces at work here. I immediately went into meditation, using the Violet Flame to surround us with protection. I kept the Violet Flame flowing.

# THIS IS A VERY IMPORTANT LIFETIME FOR YOU

Getting to Tulum was chaotic and I couldn't shake the feeling that there was something trying to prevent me from going.

I needed more help to get rid this negativity. I texted a friend in the United States while in the van. She is very intuitive and a channel. When I contacted her, she immediately responded back, as if she were waiting for my text.

I could tell by her text that she was concerned about our safety. She texted that I should shield myself well, because she was picking negative energies. Then she said they were waiting for me, so she energetically put a Merkabah and Metatron Cube around us for protection.

Without knowing the ordeal we had gone through to get to Tulum, she said *they* were trying to stop us from going there. While in the van with all this going on, I suddenly felt children in Spirit. As I continued to text my friend in the United States, she confirmed that I needed to help cross over some children from the earth plane to a higher realm. I sensed thirteen children, eleven girls and two boys.

Spirit intuitively instructed me to do this on the way to Tulum. I was not to acknowledge the negative energy trying to stop me, but should keep my focus on the children. I received information that these children had been sacrificed at Tulum, so I continued to use the Violet Flame and called on Jesus, Archangel Michael, Melchizedek, and the Golden Phoenix to help protect us all. That would allow the children to transition and keep us safe on our journey.

Now, I could feel my breathing becoming a little easier as I did this. My friend from the United States texted that she was sending a dragonfly as confirmation of the negative energies being transmuted and that the children had been successfully transitioned.

As we continued driving, I performed a cleansing, releasing, and protection meditation for the children and ourselves. I focused on the Golden Phoenix to remove the negative forces, so I could assist the children to cross over. When I saw the dragonfly cross the van window in front us, I knew it was done.

As we started to slow down, I saw our driver, Angel, pulling into a parking lot. He said, "I usually drop people off here, but I feel as though I need to walk you up to get your tickets." I felt in my heart that he knew we needed protection. Our driver was an angel sent to help and protect us.

Angel walked with us to buy our admission tickets, as we decided to get a map and tour the grounds ourselves. I decided to trust my intuition to let me know where to perform the Violet Flame.

I forgot to mention that when my friend and I were on the beach at our hotel, an iguana crept close to our chairs. I thought she was going to jump out of her skin, because she couldn't stand iguanas.

When we arrived, two items showed up at the entrance to the ruins at Tulum. First, the purple heart flowers were just like the ones I had bought earlier from our students before I left for my trip. They were growing everywhere in the gray stone here. This was Spirit confirming that I was in the right place and we were being protected.

The other thing that showed up were iguanas. I apologized to my friend for the numerous iguanas here. She cringed each time she saw an iguana, but said she was fine with it, so we walked further into the ruins. We needed to choose which path we were going to take first. I felt that we needed to go up towards the water, as I was drawn to perform the Violet Flame at the temple there. It was called The Temple of the God of the Wind. I love the Wind—it's one of my favorite elements.

We walked along the ledge and looked out over the magnificent ocean. It was truly a breathtaking view. The water had beautiful hues of blue, green, and aqua. We stood on a cliff admiring the view.

Just below us was a small beach, where a lot of commotion was going on. We didn't know what had happened until we saw a hysterical woman. We heard that she was feeding a banana to one of the iguanas and it bit her hand. What was she thinking?

My friend has a fear of iguanas, so we walked on. I was very drawn to a temple in the middle of the ruins. I could feel the intense energy drawing me to it. I knew intuitively this is why I came here. This is where I need to do the Violet Flame.

I wondered what temple this was. Intuitively I kept receiving, "Ixchel, Ixchel." A tour group was next to us, so I tried to listen to what their guide was saying to his group.

I was right—this was Ixchel's Temple, the Temple of Birthing. I felt a heaviness in my chest again and knew this was the spot. This is why I came—to transmute the energy with the Violet Flame. I kept doing it until I began to feel a release in my chest. I felt a Divine Mother connection here in this Temple. It was palpable.

Then I felt an influx of Divine love. It felt as if it was pouring in through me and expanding out from me into the energy field of the planet. I knew a portal, an interdimensional door, had been unblocked. It was reopened to allow Beautiful Christ Consciousness Energy to flow through me and fill the Temple.

> I could breathe easily again and felt a great sense of peace and unconditional love.

I could feel Mother Mary's presence was here with us. We did it—we felt a completion. At that moment, I felt an electrical jolt go through my body. The portal for Tulum was here and we were now standing in it, a cleansed portal that was reopened. The negative energies were transmuted.

We left to meet our driver, Angel, where he said he would be. Our mission was now complete. As if we hadn't received enough signs, as we were in the van going back to the hotel, a beautiful blue butterfly representing the transformation that had just taken place at Tulum flew across the front van window.

We returned to our hotel and had a great last evening at the pool. Early the next morning, we set off to the airport and made our way back home.

When I returned to work, I was interested in how my co-worker's trip to Lourdes went. She said it was an amazing trip, except that she became violently ill in the middle of it.

I asked her what day that was and she said Tuesday. When I asked if she was able to take the crystals to Mother Mary at Lourdes, she said she took them on Wednesday. She had my crystals in her pocket on Tuesday, I wondered if she was picking up on my severe illness that day. We are all connected.

For me, everything that happened on my trip made sense looking back. The woman who came up to me on the beach had crossed herself three times with the sign of the cross. This woman sensed that I needed protection.

---

> I believe she sensed Mother Mary around me and that she was preparing and protecting me for the task I had in Tulum. Mother Mary received my gift to her, the crystals that my friend placed at her feet. I know Mother Mary was there with me, guiding, healing, and protecting me in Mexico.

## CHAPTER 27

# Golden Statue

My day began with my daughter calling me, crying on the phone and wanting me to pick her up at college for the weekend. She said she needed to go to the Boston Museum of Fine Arts for her class.

I knew that was just a small part of why she was upset. She was really miserable at school and needed a break to come home. The trip from Boston to Connecticut on Friday night during rush hour would take me three hours each way, but I loved her. She knew that I would do it, because I would do anything for her.

We decided to take the train into the city Saturday morning. I had looked forward to visiting the Museum of Fine Arts, as it had been a while since I had been there. They had an Egyptian Collection that I was excited to see. I had looked forward to this, because I held guided meditations to Egypt with my clients. I have never *physically* traveled to Egypt, but through my meditations with clients, I have always felt a strong connection to that land.

I knew my daughter needed to complete her assignment *before* I could wander about in the museum. She was tasked with writing about Aphrodite in Greek Mythology. She found a few sculptures that would work, but she was still hoping to find Aphrodite's bust. As we wandered from one room to the next searching for it, we found ourselves in a magnificent Egyptian collection.

The statues of the Gods and Goddesses felt surreal, as if I had just arrived in Egypt. I was also trying to locate Isis and Thoth, but as we walked, I started feeling sick to my stomach, so I asked my daughter, "Do you feel all right?"

She said she felt like she was going to vomit. Since I did, too, I knew I had better do something quickly to transmute the energy we were feeling. I began invoking the Violet Flame. I needed to bring the violet flame up through our feet and our bodies and then expand it out into the room. This helped ease some of our discomfort, yet I felt we needed more help energetically.

I said to my daughter, "I hope you don't mind, but I need to chant the sacred sound of Hu." According to Eckankar, Hu is an ancient name for God that has been sung for thousands of years for spiritual unfoldment. As I began to chant, the two people who were in the room exited, so now we were alone to continue.

I began chanting the sound, "Huuuuuuuuuuuuu, Hu!" My intention was to set free any energies that needed to be released to the light, transmuting them with this sound using the Violet Flame.

Intuitively, I knew energy was stuck. I heard the name, Amenhotep III. As I turned towards my daughter, I saw his statue and a sarcophagus. I continued chanting this sound, until I felt a release of the physical heaviness in my body.

My daughter said she felt better, also, so the pressure was lifting. I continued invoking the Violet Flame, as my daughter had completed her assignment. Now it was time for us to leave the museum and catch that train.

That night I dreamed that a monsoon was coming. I was in an open-air temple, which has no doors. The walls were made of antique white mortar.

In this temple stood a huge 18-foot statue of an Egyptian God made of gold. The statue was facing the trees and had a body of water behind it. The statue telepathically told me to free the back of his golden heels, which reminded me of unclipping a ski boot to remove it.

I managed to remove the restraint that was holding him in place, so as his heels were released, the Golden Statue fell forward to the ground. Now that he was free, he started walking forward. It was as if he came alive once he was released. Then I woke up.

Later that year I was vacationing in Sedona. Since I planned on hiking near Boynton Canyon, I was driving in that direction for the hike. However, as I drove west, the mountains from the east called me to hike in that direction. I remembered a hiking path on Schnebly Hill.

As I pulled into the parking area, all the parking spaces appeared to be taken, except for one possibility. However, the person parked next to that last spot had to pull up just a little further. Just then, the car pulled up enough for me to navigate into this very tight spot next to him.

As I got out of my car, he asked if I wanted to hike with him. I know my friends would think I was crazy to go hiking with a stranger, but I knew I was drawn to these mountains for a reason. I said, "OK, let's hike together."

As we walked together, this man told me he was writing a book on higher consciousness. He dominated most of our conversation, coming across as if he had all the answers. He spoke about the rays of light and their meanings and that he thought we shared lifetimes in Egypt together. I sensed that he was correct, since there seemed to be at least one lifetime that I remembered.

Then he said, "Thank you."

I jokingly responded, "You're welcome."

Next he said, "I'm thanking you for releasing me and setting me free." I couldn't resist my response, his ego in this lifetime, seemed to be an authoritarian. A vision of the heels of the Egyptian

God popped into my head. Perhaps this was the golden statue in the museum that I had just freed when I was with my daughter. How could this man have known about my dream? Is he really the Golden Statue that I freed?

In that moment, I knew Spirit was showing me the importance of spiritual balance. People claiming to be highly spiritually evolved like this man are humans, so they don't hold all the answers. Everyone, including myself, is a work in progress.

This museum experience showed me that releasing a part of a soul's blocked energy can expand throughout many lifetimes. Energy and healing work can influence the past, and future through the present moment. This was confirmed, when we felt the heaviness of the energy in the museum suddenly released.

A person of higher consciousness, like the man on the hike with me, who feels like they have all the answers may not, as they could be blocking their own spiritual growth. When one doesn't evolve, it is usually because they are not aware of their need for more spiritual lessons. As they continue to create opportunities for themselves, they will learn the necessary lessons that they need to be able to grow.

> This story shows a golden thread that weaves dream time and awake time throughout our lifetimes to teach us. This is the Tapestry of Life.

CHAPTER 28

# Sand Dollar I

It was April 2014, and I had just arrived in Venice, Florida. My dad was very ill and he had just been informed by his physician that he needed emergency cardiac surgery.

When we talked with his physician, he recommended that we take him back to Boston as soon as possible to see a heart specialist. My sister back home was able to set up a meeting with a cardiac specialist at Mass General, so my dad and I planned to fly out together the next day. Fortunately, one of my brothers was able to fly down, so that he could drive our mom back home to Boston.

For the past two mornings, I would discreetly escape to the beach before everyone got up and have my early morning walk. It's what held me together. The shells on the beach were just beautiful, and it was a walk that cleared my mind, body, and soul.

When my brother arrived, I encouraged him to take a walk on the beach. Our family situation was anxiety-provoking, so we each needed to find some peace.

Upon return from my brother's walk, he showed me the most beautiful sand dollar. He shared that he found it on the beach. I couldn't believe how perfect it was. In all the times I've walked the beach, I have never found one, so I was very happy for him.

When I woke up the next morning, I thought immediately of St. Joseph. We have a history together and maybe because Joseph is a father figure and my dad was very ill, this relationship was stronger than usual. I cherished my dad and felt very drawn to pray to Joseph to watch over him.

I secretly admit that I also prayed to find a sand dollar. I know this sounds petty and I even said this to myself. However, I'm not a greedy person. I think I was looking for confirmation of some kind. Feeling a bit helpless, I needed a sign from above that all would be okay and that my dad would be okay.

It was early morning as I began my walk on the beach, before we had to leave for the airport. It appeared that I was the only one out here. As I walked further, I saw a man wading in the water. He looked like he was raking for sharks' teeth, which is a pastime well-known to Venice beachgoers.

As I drew closer, I couldn't help but stare at this handsome man. He had wavy auburn hair and piercing light-blue eyes. When I wished him good morning, he said, "Good morning, I have a gift for you."

As he made his way closer to the shore where I stood, he held out his hand and placed a sand dollar into my palm. *OMG! A beautiful sand dollar—are you kidding me?* I thought to myself, I couldn't believe it. I said, "Thank you, it's beautiful!"

I didn't know what else to do, and started walking back towards my parent's condo. I couldn't take my eyes off him. The peace and serenity that flowed from this man was glorious. I kept saying to myself, "I can't believe he gave me a sand dollar!"

It wasn't until I was close to the condo that I thought to myself, *Did this really happen? I think that was Joseph!* I looked back and couldn't see him anymore. I truly think that was Joseph.

I knew my prayers were answered. The sand dollar was my sign. Thank you, Saint Joseph! My dad had his surgery and is on the road to recovery.

## CHAPTER 29

# God Spoke to Me the Night Robin Williams Died

Since I was young, I have had experiences and dreams that have been catalysts for my spiritual awakening. I have countless numbers of journals sitting packed in boxes, which are filled with recollections of dreams and experiences. Recently, I have been guided to share these dreams in hopes of benefiting others.

One such lucid dream began when I found myself in a large high-rise hotel, decorated in gold. I was on the ninth floor of this hotel and I was drawn to the woman in this room. It turns out that she was a maid who worked there. I sensed someone had died and that this maid was helping to prepare for the funeral service.

It came to me in the dream that she was preparing the funeral for a woman who had killed herself that day. I noticed the maid filling small containers with trail mix for friends and family who would be attending her funeral, so I wanted to help. I offered to fill containers, which was an offer she gladly accepted.

As we stood across the table from each other, working together, a tall man walked past the open door. I knew somehow he was the maid's boss. When he saw that I was filling the containers, his face filled with rage. He stormed into the room and started screaming at the maid.

I looked at her, standing there, helpless to stop his ranting. I intuited that he was upset because I was helping her. Perhaps he thought that she had asked me to help. Since I felt such empathy for her, I put my hand up and told him to stop yelling at her. After all, I was the one who had offered to help.

Then my vision in this dream state shifted, so that now I was sitting in the front passenger seat of a car, and God was driving. I just knew it was God. I couldn't see Him, but I sensed Him. I felt His loving Divine presence enveloped and comforted me. My head was on His shoulder while he was driving.

I said to Him, "When I die, I would like a Mass with music—definitely *Ave Maria* and *On Eagle's Wings*." As we were driving up a dirt road, he showed me the road in my mind. It looked like we were driving up the base of the middle of a curvy line that looked a Yin/Yang symbol.

As we continued our ride, when I looked to my left, I saw an open field. When I looked to the right, I saw women and children being persecuted. It was awful—so much pain and agony. In the center of the field, a woman was being crucified, nailed to a cross. Her eyes were hollow in fear and shock and her head was bald from being torched.

Others were pillaged and looked tormented. The site was horrific with great devastation. The field they were in was covered in layers of murky water. These women and children were immersed in agony and emotional suffering—their pain was palpable.

This manifested in my body as sharp pain under my fingernails, as if pins and needles were being inserted. I knew deep down that even though I was in the car with God, a part of me knew I was also a victim out there.

Then I saw a girl running with half of her long red hair on fire. The other half of her head was already bald. She appeared to only be about ten. My heart was broken. I rolled down my window as fast as I could and yelled at the top of my lungs, "Put your head in the water, put your head in the water!"

I screamed, "Why are women and children still being persecuted?" That was when God spoke to me. He said, "What you're doing is transmuting the victimhood of the Divine Feminine!" Then I woke up.

All morning I kept thinking about what God said to me. It was the same morning that I learned Robin Williams had reportedly taken his own life. I couldn't believe it. Robin, a beloved soul who made millions of people laugh and feel better, had left us. A reminder—not all is what it seems. There had been talk about him living with a severe illness and much sadness. I felt a hole in my heart and deep sadness for such a loss. His life cut way too short.

During my daily meditation, I made a connection between Robin Williams' death and my dream. Although a woman had killed herself in my dream, I do believe God was bringing my attention to what was happening in the world. What I found out later was that Robin had been working on a movie about human trafficking and pedophilia prior to his death. That touched on a major issue regarding the persecution of women and children. Is this a coincidence? Did Robin kill himself or was he victimized for helping to bring awareness to this major issue? This is for you, the reader to decide.

What I do know is that God spoke to me that night and shared a powerful message about transmuting the victimhood of the Divine Feminine. I do believe a big part of this for me has been working with the Violet Flame of transmutation over the years. This flame is a powerful tool known for transmuting lower frequencies of energy back into higher frequencies of energy.

Was this what God was conveying
to me? I believe so. One thing I
know is that on my divine path,
I will continue to work on transmuting
the victimhood of the divine feminine.

## CHAPTER 30

# Oliver

We moved into our new house, a beautiful house that I manifested. One of my sons was having a challenge. He was in middle school and found that it was not easy to change schools and leave old friends and familiarity.

My children had always wanted a dog and I'm a dog person, too. I grew up with a dog and was lucky enough to have him for sixteen years. I had always wanted another dog, but hesitated for years, because I worked full time both as a registered nurse in a school and scheduling Reiki healings at my Wellness Center after school.

Because I was a single mom juggling work, school, activities, and homework with my three children, I felt that I couldn't take on another responsibility, like having a dog. Earlier, I did give in to getting kittens, because they are more independent than dogs. However, with my son changing schools and trying to adjust, it was time to reconsider getting a family dog.

After a family conversation and some research, we decided on getting a dog, a labradoodle. It was a beautiful spring day when we drove to Rhode Island to find our new puppy. My kids were so excited, especially my son.

When we arrived, it became a difficult decision, because all these puppies were so cute. However, when a puppy put his paw through the crate and laid it onto my son's arm, we instantly knew this was the one—he stole our hearts. My son named him, Oliver, which was a very fitting name for this adorable personality. Little did I know at the time that what I thought was a gift for my son was actually a gift for me too.

We loved Oliver, but it took a while for our kittens to get used to him. Then time passed, my son grew up, and he went to college, so Oliver and I grew closer. He reminded me of the poodle I had when growing up. My poodle was very smart and adorable, too.

I wondered if it was him coming back to us in this lifetime, because of the similarities between Oliver and my poodle. They both were very smart and exuded unconditional love. Our pets love us no matter what is going on in our lives.

I worked long hours outside the home, so I couldn't wait to get home each evening to be with this beautiful fur ball, Oliver. Every morning, Oliver would hop on the couch in his favorite spot, and look at us with his sad eyes, because we were leaving. It broke my heart to leave him.

After our cat Rocky passed, Daisy, our other cat, and Oliver bonded more. We would find Daisy licking Oliver's hair. Oliver gave us a look like, "What is she doing?" Daisy did this as if she was his mother and it was so cute to watch the two of them together.

In March of 2016, my former father-in-law, an ex-marine, was dying, so I had visited him recently. One night I had a dream of being in a warzone in the Middle East. A white wolf with blue eyes appeared on my left with my left hand in his mouth. This is something that Oliver did when we were roughhousing.

In my dream, I found myself in the mess hall. Others jumped onto a truck to be taken to the war zone. Outside the mess hall, I saw a man with a rifle carrying another man on his shoulder. I went back into the mess hall and saw the author, Wayne Dyer. He brought me two funeral mass pamphlets that had white flowers and wording on them.

I kept one of the two pamphlets, the darker one with emerald writing. The written sentiment was longer on this one. I gave the other pamphlet to the person next to me. The dream ended and I woke up.

A couple of days later, my former father-in-law passed over. This loss was sad for our family, since my kids were very close to him. When my dream came to mind, I realized it was telling me that he was about to pass.

A month had gone by and I had plans to see my parents in Florida. It had been a while since I last saw them. The challenge about going was leaving Daisy and Oliver at home, although Daisy was okay with someone coming to the house every couple of days to feed her.

However, Oliver needed to be boarded in a kennel. We had boarded him before at this kennel and they were very nice. However, this time felt different. Prior to leaving Oliver, I had recurring dreams about the cycle of life.

In the dream I was sitting on a front step surrounded by a beautiful forest. While sitting there, I saw a mouse run by. A fox appeared and caught the mouse. Shortly after that, a large wolf was chasing the fox and grabbed it.

I had difficulty watching them being hurt by other animals. However, I realized this is a part of nature, but it was difficult to witness this, even in a dream. When I woke up, I wondered why I was having these dreams. It dawned on me that I was being shown the cycle of life and reminded that everything has its time—even animals.

Sunday morning, I took Oliver to the kennel prior to my flight. I still had this unsettling feeling in my stomach. I told Oliver how much I loved him and then quickly got into my car. I needed to go to see my parents, but I had no one else to watch Oliver. I quickly tried to take my mind off leaving him and told myself that he was in good hands.

# THIS IS A VERY IMPORTANT LIFETIME FOR YOU

Shortly after arriving at my parents, I went for a walk on the beach. This was my peaceful place. As I walked, I couldn't believe my eyes. My favorite bird, the Blue Heron, was on the beach and he wasn't alone. A raven was standing next to him. When I see a single raven, it means death, so someone is going to pass. Oliver immediately came to mind. I didn't want to believe there was a connection, so I discounted the thought and kept walking.

The next day I woke up early and took my parents' dog for a walk. As I walked out the condo towards the grass, a white heron was flying circles above me. I quickly rushed the dog back to the condo. When I ran into the house, I saw that my mother was on the phone.

I suddenly felt panic and turned to my parents and said, "It's Oliver, he died." My mother handed me the phone.

I heard my son say, "Mom, you need to sit down."

I said, "It's Oliver, I know he died. I saw the white heron flying above me, which was symbolic of his passing," I sobbed. My son told me that he had died that morning.

Crying, I told him Oliver is our baby, our love, so how could this be? My heart went out to my son, it was not easy for him. From the time my son was nine years old, Oliver was his puppy. However, the two of us were so close, my kids referred to him as my puppy husband. I hung up and then told my parents that I had to go home. They understood, so my mom drove me to the airport.

I couldn't stop crying over Oliver being gone. I felt guilty leaving him and wondered why I had left him to go to my parents. Looking back, there were signs something was happening, but now I realized what those signs meant.

On the plane home, I picked one of my angel cards from the deck. The card read, "I am thinking of you." Then it gave the message: "This is a message from heaven that a loved one who has passed over loves you and is thinking of you."

Although the message was comforting, I cried even harder. The song *Babe* by Styx played on the radio while I was driving home from the airport. I knew this song was Oliver sending me another message:

> Babe I'm leaving, I must be on my way ... but I'll be lonely without you, but need your love to see me through, so please believe me, my heart is in your hands and I'll be missing you.

When I returned home, my son and I went to our vet's office and did what was needed. It was a devastating time in our lives. Daisy the cat was looking for Oliver and wondering where he was. It was sad to watch her searching for him. As time passed, it became a little easier, although I would still cry—I miss him deeply.

More signs from Oliver continued to appear. When I went to Sedona with my cousin to attend a workshop was one example. While waiting for the workshop to start, a woman behind me tapped me on the shoulder. She asked me if I had a big white dog. When I said, "Yes," I also added, "He's in heaven."

She said, "Well, right now he's with you under your chair."

Although I couldn't see him, I said, "Thank you, Oliver, for your presence—I love you."

Next year, during my vacation, I went to visit my parents in Florida. I hadn't been there since Oliver's passing, so I knew it would be a difficult reminder of that time, but I knew I would be okay.

My mother was watching an old black and white movie with a golden retriever in it that was killed. Horrified I said, "I can't watch this."

I decided to leave to walk on the beach, as I needed a break. Once I was down by the water, I looked up at the clouds and couldn't believe my eyes. It was Oliver's face coming through the clouds. I quickly tried to get a picture on my phone before the cloud formation changed. I could see the pupil in one of his eyes.

> Thank you, my beloved Oliver for sending this message from above. You are amazing, a Master Being of unconditional love.

I believe Oliver was one of my teachers in this lifetime. He assisted me in healing my heart, so I could help others heal theirs. This was a message to me to continue my healing work with others. I know Oliver is with me in Spirit. When the song "Babe" comes on the radio, I know it's Oliver is talking to me.

Looking back, Oliver made sure I wasn't there when he passed. He knew it would be impossible for me to let him go, so it would have been more difficult than it already was, if I had been there. I love you, Oliver, for your presence in our life and I am forever great~full.

In the prior mess hall dream, I was given two funeral mass pamphlets. I didn't realize at the time that these pamphlets were symbolizing and preparing me for not only my former father-in-law's passing, but also for losing Oliver. Dreams, intuition, and signs are guidance and messages, if we open our awareness to the possibility.

# CHAPTER 31

# The Healing of a Presidential Candidate

In dreamtime, I'm standing near Harold's Square in New York City on a busy street. As I look around, I can see and hear a lot of hustle and bustle of people. Then I noticed the firehouse across the street.

Shortly after discovering where I was, I saw a huge square ambulance come barreling out of the firehouse. It attempted to turn, but flipped over with sirens and lights flashing. It had crashed right in front of me. I wondered where that ambulance was going.

In the next scene, I'm standing on the lowest floor of a hotel parking garage. The garage appeared vacant, except for a black truck. It was alarming, because a truck had fallen on top of a man.

No one was around except my friend, who is spiritual and does Reiki. We needed to get the truck off this man. His head and torso were visible, though the truck had fallen onto his abdomen and legs, pinning him down.

We needed to act quickly because he was hemorrhaging and bleeding out. I felt a rush of adrenaline, the needed fight or flight response, and then together, my friend and I lifted the truck off him. *Was this where the ambulance was going before it flipped over?*

I looked down at the man who was pinned under the truck and realized that he was one of the presidential candidates. I was not voting for him, so the thought crossed my mind—should I help him? However, I am an energy healer, so I needed to help him.

I instructed my friend to perform Reiki on his feet and legs, while I worked on his abdomen to stop the bleeding. He was talking nonstop, so I turned to him and said, "Be quiet and focus," as he needed to reserve his energy. After some time, I saw the internal bleeding was finally under control. When the ambulance arrived, I let the EMTs take over.

Through this dream state experience, I learned not to be swayed by how the media portrays people, including presidential candidates. It was important for me to see this man as a human being and look beyond the media's character manipulation of him. After this dream, a couple of years later, I discovered all the good this same presidential candidate did for the world.

## CHAPTER 32

# Padre Pio

I don't really know the exact date that Padre Pio came into my life, but it was during one of my many trips to the North End in Boston. My favorite place is the Peace Garden at St. Leonard's Church. There stands a tall golden statue of a man in a robe with opened arms. I didn't know who he was initially, but the energy I felt coming from this statue was palpable.

It was on that day that I asked someone standing next to me, "Who is this statue commemorating?"

They answered, "Padre Pio, the Italian saint. He had the stigmata of Jesus." This was my first introduction to this man, a Saint, who changed my life forever!

Each time I came into town, I would go over to visit with my favorite saint. Well, I have a few, but Padre Pio has a very special place in my heart. I would pray to him and call upon him in my healing sessions.

In September of 2016, I saw on television that Padre Pio's heart, a relic, was coming to Boston. I couldn't believe it. That is so weird. After researching, I learned that when Padre Pio passed over, his physical body never decomposed, which is termed incorruptible. This is how the friars traveled with his heart to Boston.

A friend and I decided to go in on a Wednesday night. It was taking place in a church in the South End of Boston. Wednesday was the only night I could go into town, so I met my friend and we drove in together.

We heard that the lines were going to be really long and to expect a wait. However, we had no problems. We parked easily, stood in line, and took in the experience. The light filtering through the stained glass was breathtaking.

As we made our way closer to the altar area, there stood a large portrait of Padre Pio. The light was shining down on him just perfectly, especially the violet light. I then brought my attention back to the people in front of me in line. I noticed the few people before us were kissing the glass case, which was holding his heart.

*What should I do?* I asked myself, and as clear as day, I heard an inner voice say, "You're a healer—put your hands up to it."

I didn't know what to expect, but there I was, right in front of this glass case being held by a Friar. I put my hands up to either side of the case and instantly felt chills running up and down my body. I took a moment to thank Padre Pio, as tears rolled down my face.

Next, I stepped out of the line to get a closer look at his portrait. All I could see was the light coming down through the windows. Beautiful bright golden white and violet light filled the church.

Then my friend came up and asked, "Do you want to go to the gift shop?"

I agreed, so we walked to the back of the church and bought prayer cards and medals to take with us to remember this auspicious moment in time. I didn't realize the effect this had on me, though I knew it touched me deeply.

The next day, I rose early for work at the hospital. My day was filled with Reiki sessions for patients going through radiation for cancer treatment. My first patient was a massage therapist, who had undergone a mastectomy. She shared that she had severe pain and lymphedema, with so much swelling that she wasn't able to lift or move her arm.

I don't make claims to patients, so all I could say to her was for her to climb up on the table and try to relax. Then I proceeded as I normally do during a session, combining Reiki with relaxation techniques. This includes soft music, a passive muscle relaxation, a guided visualization of violet light filling all the cells in her body, and a journey to the beach.

As I stood next to her, my left hand was above her head and my right hand was placed over her heart. I could feel the energy throughout my body, so I knew Reiki was flowing through her. I was in this position for about a minute. Suddenly, I felt something profound happening. Sometimes I can see, while other times I can hear and feel, but this time I just knew something was happening. And then she screamed.

I stopped to ask if she was OK. She said, "A man in a brown robe just put his hand through my chest and pulled out my pain. "Look," she said.

She proceeded to wave around her affected arm, when previously she had very little movement in it. She moved it effortlessly, waving it around to show me. I couldn't believe my eyes.

Then I said, "Wait." I ran to my bag and pulled out a prayer card of Padre Pio and brought it over to her. "Is this him?"

She yelled, "That's him—he's the one!"

I proceeded to tell her about my visit the night before to see the relic of Padre Pio's heart. I shared that I had put my hands up to the glass case that held his precious heart.

We both were dumbfounded. We knew she had just experienced a miracle. Working in a medical facility, there's not too many people to whom you can tell this story, because it doesn't go over very well.

# THIS IS A VERY IMPORTANT LIFETIME FOR YOU

I went out to the waiting room for my next patient. It was her first Reiki session on our radiation floor. I had met her about a month ago upstairs on the medical oncology floor. The problem I have working in the energy is that I forget what people say sometimes and what happens in many of our sessions.

She had stage three breast cancer and just had a mastectomy. I didn't say anything to her about my previous patient's experience. During our session, I was standing on the patient's right side, in the same position as I was for the previous patient.

She said to me, "Nancy, this is going to sound crazy, but a man in a brown robe is standing next to you." Although I told her nothing sounds crazy to me, I still couldn't believe what I was hearing. I hadn't said a word to her about the previous patient's experience.

I immediately went to my bag again and showed her the picture of Padre Pio. She said, "Yes, that's him."

This is very unreal—it's unbelievable. Then I proceeded to tell her about placing my hands on the glass case that held Padre Pio's heart. I also shared what just happened with the patient before her and then we both cried.

When I sat back down on the stool above her head, I noticed there was a face, his face—Padre Pio's face was staring back at me from the Himalayan salt lamp on the table. I said to her, "Look! Look at the lamp! Do you see his face? There's a heart on the top of his head,"

She said, "Oh, my God, I see it—I see his face and the heart!"

I had more patients that day. No one else mentioned seeing Padre Pio, but we did. It was later that evening, when I received a call on my cell phone from my second patient.

She said she was sorry to bother me, but she saw my phone number on my business card and had to tell me, "When I came home, I picked up my mail. In it was an envelope from the Padre

Pio Foundation. Never before had I ever received anything from them. It's all confirmation from Spirit!" It all really happened. That night before bed, I said a prayer of gratitude to the Saint Padre Pio!

> Both women experienced a
> miracle that day and
> I am forever great~full
> to have witnessed it.
> Thank you Padre Pio!

## CHAPTER 33

# The Shroud

I am here again in my favorite spot in Sedona, sharing its magic with my cousin. She lost her husband this past year and needed some magic put back in her life. Out of anywhere I had ever been, I knew this would be the place to give her a sign from her husband.

We decided to meditate at Oak Creek, overlooking the beautiful Cathedral Rock. While meditating I kept sensing the shroud of Jesus, but I'm not sure why. It could have been something about the resurrection. This spot is where I have meditated and prayed to Yeshua, Jesus, in the past. One trip, I fell fully clothed into the creek. I knew I needed to be cleansed, but didn't expect *that* to happen.

While there, I asked my cousin to take a picture of me. I was drawn to have her take one in that exact spot this time. After she took the picture, we walked further on to another area of prayer rock statues. This is where my cousin had her own experience with a butterfly.

A butterfly wouldn't leave her alone. It followed her for several minutes, flying all around her and landing on her. She saw this butterfly as a transformation and knew it was a sign from her husband. Next, we went to a metaphysical store that has some amazing crystals.

As we made our way into the store, the first thing that caught my attention was a prayer card with the shroud of Jesus on it. I had to have it. Prior to entering the store, I had shared with my cousin what I received in meditation about the shroud, so when I showed her the card, she said, "You have to get that!"

I knew it, also, so I included it in my shopping basket that was already filled with crystals. After shopping, we decided to get a bite to eat and then call it an evening, as we had been up for sunrise to capture the beautiful colors as the sun's rays danced over the Red Rocks.

When we finally arrived back in our hotel room, I decided to look at the pictures I had taken that day. Glancing over them, I noticed something strange. My cousin had taken three pictures of me with my phone camera at Cathedral Rock. Two pictures looked normal, but one looked like I had red dirt all over the lower part of me, like I had rolled in the red dirt.

However, I could see the image of Jesus on the Cross on my legs in the picture. At another angle it looked like the face of Jesus. I showed my cousin the pictures and she also saw the images.

We couldn't believe our eyes. Seeing these pictures confirmed the shroud information I had received in meditation. How can this be—what does this mean?

Once I returned home from our trip, I had some time to reflect on the messages I was receiving from Yeshua. What is the shroud and what does it mean? Here are my thoughts:

There are many pictures and images of Jesus (Yeshua) in our time. However, photography wasn't present in the time he lived. The first true image of Jesus in his lifetime was imprinted on the shroud. The shroud carries an energetic imprint of the man, Jesus. There is more to us than our physical bodies.

The shroud is also symbolic of a veil. The veil between heaven and earth is getting thinner. As a collective and individually, we are raising our energetic frequency. As this occurs, our intuitive senses are heightened; increasing the possibilities of receiving messages from Spirit and our loved ones who have transitioned.

I also realized that my cousin had received a much-needed sign in this magical place in Sedona. She experienced a butterfly following and dancing around her, which is a beautiful sign of transformation. When the butterfly appeared to her, intuitively she knew it was a message. She shared the feeling of peace in her heart and knew her husband was letting her know he was OK.

> This was a reminder that our soul lives on, even after leaving our physical bodies. We are eternal beings. Thank you, Yeshua, and magical Sedona.

# CHAPTER 34

# Padre Pio's Relics and the Walkway

It was October 1, 2017, as I made my way down to Narragansett, Rhode Island.

Padre Pio's relic was coming to a church there. I wasn't sure what relic would be presented. The last time in Boston, it was his heart. It didn't matter to me. The only thing that mattered was that I was there to share my gratitude for the miraculous healings he had already bestowed on so many.

I previously planned to meet my friend, who had experienced one of the miraculous healings by Padre Pio at the hospital. We became close friends after our magical experience together. When we heard his relic was coming to Rhode Island, we both knew we needed to be there to show our gratitude.

As I was getting closer to the church, I noticed signs directing people to park in assigned lots for the event. I finally pulled up to an attendant parked at an elementary school parking lot.

He asked me if I wanted to take the shuttle or walk through the Padre Pio walkway after parking my car. Well, that was easy—of course, I chose the Padre Pio Walkway. I thought to myself, an invitation for miracles.

# THIS IS A VERY IMPORTANT LIFETIME FOR YOU

It was a cloudy, damp day. As I began walking towards the path, I noticed being surrounded by tall trees and thick foliage. I had to step onto small rocks over a stream and then onto the pathway. I couldn't help but notice the sign on my right. It was a sign with a red arrow pointing upward, stating, "Padre Pio Walkway." I immediately took a picture of the sign.

As I continued walking, bright, golden white light began streaming through the trees in front of me. It was surreal and magical. I felt goosebumps all over my body. It wasn't a long path, but as I approached the end, the church was straight in front of me. Booths were outside with people selling Padre Pio prayer cards and medals, along with blessed rosary beads.

One attendant said that the Mass was going to start shortly, so we should go inside. She then shared that following the Mass, people could visit the relics. When I turned around, I called to my friend and we went in together.

When it was my turn to stand in front of the altar where the three relics resided, I noticed three pieces of cloth with blood on them. The people were sharing that Padre Pio had worn them over his stigmata bloody wounds. It's kind of strange wanting to be around a relic like that. However, I believe they carry the energy of Saint Padre Pio, who was one of the very few that had the Stigmata of Christ. As I looked upon his photograph on the altar with gratitude, chills flooded my body. This is surreal.

My turn at the altar ended and I noticed my friend was now at the back of the church waiting for me. She had already been through the line. While exiting to the outside of the church, we shared our own experiences with each other.

I asked if she had taken the walkway, she said she didn't know about it. I shared with her about my magical experience. I asked her if she wanted to experience it by walking with me to my car. I told her that I would drive her to her car after. She loved the idea.

As we walked through the magical walkway, she shared a deep sense of peace and we both felt the presence of Padre Pio with us. As I dropped her off at her car, we sat and wept together. We both were so happy and great~full for the experience.

It wasn't until later when I got home, I noticed a couple of things in my pictures. Firstly, the light streaming through the trees was a brilliant white. It looked like the Holy Spirit. Secondly, I noticed Padre Pio's face in the trees. Who would ever believe this?

> When I witness mystical things in my photographs, I know it's Spirit. A message coming into the here and now confirmed Padre Pio's continued presence around us.

## CHAPTER 35

# A Girl in Her Bright Yellow Plane

In dreamtime, I found myself standing on an airport runway looking up at the pilot's door. It's a small bright yellow plane with an open cockpit. It looked like a biplane from the 1940s.

I was talking to a teenage girl with blonde pigtails. She looked like a young Julia Stiles. The girl told me she decided to leave her town, because she was being called to go to two different destinations.

I noticed the girl's mother on the tarmac as we arrived. I observed myself leaning up against the door of the plane, telling her that she had enough fuel to reach one destination, possibly two.

The teen girl wanted me to give her a hug before she left. I asked, "Don't you want a hug from your mother on the tarmac?"

She said, "No, I want you to hug me." Then I woke up.

I have had many symbolic dreams like this over the years—dreams that held messages for me. In analyzing this particular dream, I knew this was my inner child, needing love, strength, and encouragement to do what she's always wanted to do in her heart.

I had been dreaming of moving to Sedona ever since I had visited there in 2001. I was thinking at the time that Sedona was the definite destination of my dream, until a month later, when the dream's message took another direction—you might say a change in flight plan. This was a realization I wasn't aware of at the time, thinking that my story was complete. However, to my amazement and my sincere gratitude, it was not.

My dad was coming to the end of his life. I visited my parents' home in Florida during the February 2019 school vacation, a home that I've mentioned in past experiences. My siblings and I were taking turns, helping and being a support in any way we could to both parents.

My mother was overtired and overwhelmed. We had hired caregivers to come into our home to help, and they were wonderful, but Dad needed full-time care. He was able to feed himself, if it was set up for him. Most of his waking time was spent in a wheelchair now.

I love my dad deeply. He's a man of integrity and honor, so I knew this was very difficult for him. One of his caregivers was ill a week prior to my arrival. She had been coughing on the job, so my mom sent her home, but then Dad developed a cough.

Thank God, I was able to help fill in. Dad had gotten used to his children being able to help him and assist with his care. We did the best we could under the circumstances—this is what we do for our loved ones.

This week was difficult, as we were coming to the point of having to make a crucial decision. Dad needed around-the-clock care, and it was becoming overwhelming and exhausting for mom. It was taking its toll on her. The night before I headed home, my mom asked me to visit long-term care facilities with her.

It wasn't a pleasant task, as I didn't want him to be in such a place. I was afraid if he knew this was the plan, he would give up his will to live, but what other choice did we have? My sister talked about moving Dad back up north and having him stay with her, which we have done in the past. However, at this point, it would be way too much, since he now needed full-time care.

The woman who was showing us around the facility mentioned he could have photos of us to make it feel more like home. The tears rolled down my face—I couldn't hold them back. This wouldn't be his home—not even close, but we didn't have to decide right now.

Before I left for the airport, Dad was still able to converse. He was sitting in his wheelchair watching golf, when he asked if I was coming back. I said, "Yes, in April."

I knew he was sad that I was leaving. I felt the same way, but I also felt the comfort in knowing my sister was coming down in a few weeks.

The next day when I arrived home, my mother called and said Dad was taken to the hospital by ambulance. His cough worsened and she was worried that it was pneumonia. Pneumonia is the number one cause of death in a patient with Parkinson's Disease. The doctors diagnosed bronchitis, as well as a severe urinary tract infection. He was administered antibiotics and fluids.

However, there was a problem—Dad had already been in hospice care. Once you are there, they don't do things for patients to prolong life. I had mixed feelings about our decision for him to be in hospice, as he still had life within him. I knew he wasn't ready to transition.

The hospital staff offered the option of sending him home or he could choose to go for a five-day respite in a hospice house. In reviewing our options we knew our mom wasn't able to take care of him at home, as he was very weak and needed help around the clock. Therefore, we had to choose respite care for him.

My sister decided to travel to my parents when she learned that his condition was deteriorating. She called me a couple of days after she arrived and said it didn't look good. He was declining quickly.

I said I wanted to come down. My oldest brother hadn't seen Dad since the fall. He needed to be there for sure, so she called him and he made arrangements to go.

I spoke to my sister again and she said my mother needs me after my brother leaves. In my heart, I wanted to be there now, so I tried to find coverage for my school nursing job. However, I was having difficulty finding someone. I felt trapped and didn't know what to do, although my intuition knew exactly what to do.

My sister said that she could put the phone up to my dad and I could talk to him. As I sobbed, I told him how much I loved him. He had been a great father and grandfather, but it was okay for him to go.

Sunday morning, we were supposed to have a major snowstorm that evening, with over a foot and a half of snow. When I spoke to my sister, she said my brother had arrived the night before. They thought it would be any day now that my dad would pass.

I talked with one of my best friends and she said it was time for me to go be with him. She reminded me that I wouldn't want to have any regrets not being there. She also reminded me that a big part of my healing work has been helping people pass over, so I knew I had to be there for him.

I called everyone I knew who could cover my schedule. I finally called my boss, she said just go—they would figure it out. I immediately looked up flights leaving before the snow, but they were all too expensive and had connecting flights.

# THIS IS A VERY IMPORTANT LIFETIME FOR YOU

At last, one flight came up with a direct flight to Fort Myers on Spirit Airlines for a reasonable price, which left in four hours. I booked it immediately and called my daughter to drive me to the airport. She said that she would do anything she could to help me get there in time. She knew how much I cherished my father.

I made it to the airport, but then there was a delay. I panicked, as I knew I had to get there before he passed. I wanted to tell him one more time I loved him, and that transitioning is beautiful—he would be okay. Flights were starting to get cancelled, but mine was not.

My dad was from a scientific background. He wasn't religious, but he knew I was spiritual, like his mother. After takeoff, I started listening to *Chanting of the Angels from Atlantis*. I had made an appointment for having an intuitive reading, but it was too soon. However, I had received the music as part of the package a month earlier from the reader.

I remembered I had booked the session for Tuesday evening, March 5th. It was okay that I wasn't home, because it was a reading over the phone. As the plane landed, I felt a deep sense of peace and strength come over me. I knew I would make it there in time to see Dad. I had texted a driver who had taken us in the past to pick me up. When I let him know what was happening, he said he would be there. He took me straight to the hospice house.

My brother and mother were there waiting for me. They had let the staff know that I would be flying in and arriving after regular visiting hours. My brother informed me Dad hadn't opened his eyes at all. As I approached his side, I kissed him and let him know that I was here. I told him how much I loved him and that it was okay for him to go. I silently prayed he could hear me.

I shared with him that loved ones and angels surrounded him. I reassured him that Mom would be okay. I emphasized that we would take good care of her, but she is a strong woman.

As I kissed him goodbye, I told him he was a great father and grandfather. It was then that he opened one eye. I knew he knew I was there.

Thank you, God! Thank you for getting me there in time. We were trying not to sob. We all shared stories, knowing in our hearts he could hear us. It was then I received a message. The girl in her bright yellow plane was me getting a direct flight with Spirit Airlines, a bright yellow plane, to be with my dad before he passed. Spirit Airlines has bright yellow planes. Little did I know at the time that this was the definite destination in my dream—well, one of two destinations.

The evening of my dad's passing, March 5th, I had my previously scheduled reading with a well-known voice coach and intuitive. He couldn't believe the synchronicities and validated that I helped my dad in his transition process, along with the angels. He also confirmed a future move to Sedona, as my other destination, which is now part of my divine soul's mission.

---

> I am forever great~full to have had you as my dad. Love you forever, Dad!

---

## CHAPTER 36

# Sand Dollar II

My dad had just passed over to Spirit early this morning. I headed to the beach to clear my head and to look for a sign from above. I was praying for a sign, but not just any sign—I wanted to find a sand dollar, as a sand dollar represents messages from Spirit to me.

As I walked, grieving a deep loss, tears rolled down my face. My eyes were blurry from crying and my hair kept getting in my eyes from the wind, making it more difficult to find a sand dollar.

The man I idolized, loved, and cherished has passed. I know in my heart he's just changed form, but his physical presence isn't here. I'm so sad. I continue to pray for a sign. "Dad, please send me a sand dollar."

I have searched before and have never been able to find one. There was one time when a man named Joseph gifted me a sand dollar. I spoke about this in my earlier writings in *Sand Dollar I*.

I continued to pray with each step I took. I was coming to the end of the beach to the jetty, feeling a bit despaired. I looked down at the sand and there it was—a sand dollar—a small fully intact sand dollar! I was so excited and elated to see a sign from above.

I took a picture of it and then put the sand dollar safely into my sweatshirt pocket, so as not to break it. Then, I stepped further and saw another one! I took pictures of each one.

I will cherish these sand dollars forever. I am very great~full for these sand dollars, as they are a gift from above. Thank you, Daddy. I love you so much.

CHAPTER 37

# A Shaman, My Dad, and Sophia

My friend called and shared that a Shaman was coming into town and would be staying with her for a day. She invited me to join with others to do a group meditation and a journey. I had studied Shamanism in the past and some of my shamanic experiences have been a big part of my self-discovery. I immediately accepted her invitation.

The energy of the group was amazing all day. We journeyed and did energy work. The Shaman also taught us some energetic techniques. It was getting late, so everyone had left except the Shaman, my friend and me. My friend was extremely tired and fell asleep on the couch.

The Shaman turned to me and sensed there was something more I wanted to work on. He asked if I wanted to journey with him. I said, yes, because I wondered if we could make sure my dad was in a good place on the other side, as he had transitioned earlier that year.

Dad was an electrical engineer and came from a scientific background, but he wasn't religious or spiritual. Prior to his passing, I remembered him saying he hoped he'd go to heaven, but wasn't sure if it existed, since he had his doubts. I tried to share my belief in the afterlife, but Dad needed more proof.

The Shaman said we could do this together, but that it might get intense. I didn't care, because I wanted to do this for my dad. I felt so high energetically after the shamanic experience that day, I thought I could do anything at that point.

We began our journey deep into the unconscious world. I followed the Shaman's lead. I wanted to help Dad raise his frequency to elevate his plane of existence, if it was for his highest good.

As we began our journey, it felt like my dad was at a door to another level. When I asked for his permission to do this, I received a yes. The Shaman began by taking me on the journey. I don't remember much about what happened next, but I could feel energy unlike anything I've ever felt. It was like we were swimming in swirling liquid. The energy continued to deepen as we journeyed.

Our starting point of the journey was like being in the deep end of a pool, but on the bottom. As we progressed, we kept rising higher and higher and the energy felt lighter. I was clearer and light radiated outward to my dad. We were now complete, according to the Shaman. It felt complete to me too.

I thanked him for doing this for my dad and me. It was late, so I needed to head home and go to bed. I didn't remember any dreams that night. However, the next night he gave me the confirmation I was seeking. I had a visit from Dad. It wasn't a dream, but a visitation. He was standing in my room, as he spoke three words to me. He announced in a loud voice, "You are Sophia."

I knew then my father got it, because he saw me for who I am spiritually. For many years, he was perplexed and didn't understand the spiritual path I was on. Shaking his head, he would say I was just like his mother, though he clearly didn't understand her either. My paternal grandmother for whom I was named was very spiritual. He called me Sophia, who is the goddess of wisdom and the feminine aspect of the Divine mother.

I know the journey the Shaman and I went on helped raise my dad's consciousness. This was a gift for both my dad and me. This guided shamanic journey helped Dad find a deeper understanding of who I am. It also filled a void in my being, so now I felt complete in Dad's love for me.

> I was elated to experience this with my dad. We helped each other. I am forever great~full for the Shaman who came into town that day.
> I strongly believe this was all divinely orchestrated.

# CHAPTER 38

# Past Life in Athens, Greece

During a past life session, I was in Athens, Greece. I was a Grecian dressed in a golden headdress and held a high position. I had difficulty dealing with the suffering of others, so in that lifetime, I carried extensive knowledge of healing techniques. I learned the importance of moving beyond the suffering of others.

This meant I was to dig deep into my heart to understand the complexity of suffering physically, emotionally, mentally, and spiritually. I learned in this Grecian lifetime that as a being of light, we are the light, the conduit for healing. Healing is not about us healing a person. It is about the healer being the conduit through which energy flows and the person receiving the healing activates their own healing ability innately.

It's not the healer's responsibility. The healer steps out of the way to let the universal life force move through us to the person. As a conduit of healing light, the techniques I used in this Grecian lifetime were working with the healing benefits of minerals and crystals.

A message came forth from Amethyst informing me that I was going to need her for the next step in my current life. The mineral kingdom guides me as it works through me in my current life as a healer. The amethyst relates to the pineal gland and the crown chakra promoting the expansion of higher consciousness. This was important, as it was a piece to the next level on my journey as a healer in my current life.

As my past life session continued, there was a shift that brought in a spirit guide, who was Clara Barton. She was a humanitarian and the nurse who founded the American Red Cross in the 1800s. After she came through, I realized she was helping me with clients who had trauma, showing me how to help someone navigate through the process of healing.

She is reminding me to get out of the way and just be the higher frequency. She went on to show that I was the channel for the healing energy and the responsibility lies with them.

This was confirmation that in both lifetimes, I was not to take on the responsibility of others' suffering—I was to be the conduit of light for the healing to take place.

Clara also reminded me of the importance of working with herbs, plants, and the element of water. I continue to use these healing techniques in my current healing practice with results.

## CHAPTER 39

# Blue Avians

It was a late afternoon in Sedona. I was hiking with a few friends up to Thunder Mountain to catch sunset. My friend, Kaveri, and I were taking our time, hiking further behind the other three.

We were discussing ETs and angels. Kaveri shared how she felt more connected to ETs, but for me, it was angels. It was just after saying this to her, when I looked up at the red rocks and saw two blue beings.

"Look, look up there. What's that?" I asked. It looked like two blue ETs. We yelled up to the others to look up. These beings were located on a huge red rock formation that looked like an ET. I quickly pulled out my phone and began taking pictures and a video. My hands were shaking uncontrollably.

One of the beings was very tall, while the other was shorter in appearance. They both had royal blue, large helmet-type heads, and lighter blue bodies. When they moved, it reminded me of those action figures, the Transformers.

They looked like large birds in one view, but then more human-like in another. Two people in our group shared they thought they might be amazing rock climbers, but three of us did not. We knew in our hearts they were ETs. We tried getting closer, but then they were gone.

No one had a zoom camera. I felt both anxious and excited seeing these beings. My intuition told me they were benevolent beings watching over us.

We were very excited to witness this in person. Each of us shared how we had seen spaceships in the skies over Sedona, but never ETs in person. During our hike back, we stopped to look at our pictures. When I looked at the video recording I had taken, it was wiped out in the middle. It was a 26-second-long video, starting at 1 second and ended at 26 seconds with nothing in-between. I felt these blue beings didn't want a video of them.

I was able to get a few photos though. In the background of one photo, it looked like a small spacecraft. One of our friends sent the photos to Mufon (Mutual UFO Network) to see if they could identify these beings. According to Mufon, the photos weren't clear enough to identify. It really didn't matter, as we knew—this experience was meant for us.

In talking with other friends in Sedona and doing research, the description of what we saw aligned with the Blue Avian race. According to one source, the Era of Light, Blue Avians are a benevolent humanoid, bird-like extraterrestrial race. They are here for peace and provide protection for humanity. The Blue Avians are helping us with ascension and assisting us with raising our frequency as a collective and Mother Earth (Gaia) herself. There are some beings who don't want this to happen.

> The Blue Avians are a part of the Alliance team helping humanity to free themselves from the control of negative forces. Thank you, Blue Avians, for watching over us.

## CHAPTER 40

# Della Plant Spirit's Message

I was gifted two beautiful plants from a friend who was moving. I helped her pack her belongings for the move.

In dreamtime I saw a plant spirit being. It was bright green about a foot tall and had a green body, head, arms, legs, and green petals all over her body. She was poking me and trying to attach herself to me, but I wasn't letting her. I knew somehow, she was trying to tell me something, but I didn't know what.

I could feel her piercing pokes on my thigh. After that I woke up. Later that day I was sitting and looking at one of the plants I was gifted. I named her Della. I noticed one of her petals had been pierced in the center by a needle of the cactus that shared the same pot.

I jumped up and immediately removed the piercing needle gently, as if this was a surgical procedure. Then I did a healing on her. I knew then that she came to me in my dream state to get help. She wanted my immediate attention and response. She was poking me, so I wouldn't forget when I woke up. I was in amazement, but the story doesn't end there.

What I've found over the years is that usually this is a two-way street. What happened next shows how I was helped by Della.

I went to drive my car to the store, when I noticed my tire light was on. I wasn't sure exactly what was wrong with my tires, but knew I should take it somewhere and at least get my air pressure checked.

In doing so, the technician at the tire place said I had a huge nail in one of my tires, which he removed and then fixed.

There it was. Della was poking me in dreamtime and I realized when I woke up, the cactus was poking her. She helped me by alerting me that I was also being poked. It wasn't a surprise to find out I had a nail poking my tire. We are being approached in dreamtime but the messages apply to our waking time.

## CHAPTER 41

# Mercury in Retrograde and Monument Valley

It was 3:30 in the morning and I was off on a long road trip to meet my daughter. I've done similar trips before from Sedona to Colorado. I knew it would be a twelve-hour drive through the desert. My daughter and I are meeting in Colorado Springs for a fun mother-daughter weekend. I was very excited.

Prior to leaving, I made sure my car had an oil change and was ready for the long drive. Mercury is in retrograde, so anything can happen. It's believed this is a time when communications can be interrupted. It's also a time to slow down what you're doing and tune into yourself.

Before leaving the house, I put my money, driver's license, and bank credit card into a black cloth fanny pack. I also had a purse with a wallet, another credit card, and some cash. However, most of my money was in the fanny pack that I would keep on me.

I asked my angels for protection on the road. Then I surrounded myself in light. I do this every time I get into my car. These prayers include sending light and protection to other people, animals, and cars on the road. After I was all set to go, I started driving. I decided to stop at the last exit in Flagstaff to top off my gas tank. I knew there would be fewer gas stations as I continued on from here.

Before I left home and for comfort when driving, instead of putting my fanny pack with my money and credit cards around my waist, I decided to fold it and put it in the inside pocket of my jacket. I had a fleeting thought that the pocket wasn't a genuine pocket, but I dismissed it. Back in the car, the GPS was set and I was headed towards Monument Valley. It's one of my favorite places. I make sure to pass through there when traveling to Utah or Colorado.

The drive was wonderful. I made it to Monument Valley in time for a beautiful sunrise. The photographs will be spectacular. I began pulling over at spots and taking pictures of the light on the red rock formations. I viewed nature's beauty with the snowcapped mountains in the distance. I got my camera and took photos with both the camera and my phone to capture these amazing views. The best is when I see Monument Valley from a distance on the Utah side. I like to stand in the middle of the road and take photos as long as cars aren't coming.

It was time to get back into the car and continue my journey. I had a thought to check to ensure I had my fanny pack and belongings. However, as I went into my jacket pocket, it was empty. Upon examining my pocket further, I realized it wasn't a pocket. I must have slid the fanny pack through this opening to the lining of my jacket. I anxiously looked everywhere in my car to see if it fell onto the seat or floor, but it was nowhere to be found.

What am I going to do? I tried to think of everywhere I had stopped. I had my bank card, money, and license in there. I had thought to call the bank, but I had no phone service. Panicked, I drove to each stop that I had pulled over to take photos.

When I stopped, there was a man in a van. I had asked if he had seen a fanny pack, but he said no. His response threw me further into a state of panic and fear. I will need my ID for the hotel check-in.

I continued to drive to each view area, pull over and look on the ground, but I didn't find it. Finally, I drove my car up and down the roadway, losing hope. I even went back to the last stop where I initially realized it was missing.

Dismayed I decided to concede and continue driving to Utah and on to Colorado. I heard an angelic voice inside my mind that told me to turn around and go towards the police station in Kayenta.

Kayenta is the small town I drive through before arriving in Monument Valley. I hadn't thought to let the police know, but I had nothing to lose. I followed the angelic advice, turned my car around, and headed to Kayenta.

I drove past all the spots I had already checked for my fanny pack. I drove a little further and then remembered, I had stopped to take a photo of the mountain. I drove into the pull-over spot to look and found nothing on the ground. Since more people were beginning to pull over, I got back into my car and continued to drive to the next pull-over spot. I wondered if this was the first stop I had made.

I pulled in and got out of my car. As I looked around, I saw what looked like a soft black mask people wore during COVID. I went over to it and sure enough it was my black folded fanny pack with everything in it. I cried tears of gratitude. I thanked my angels and couldn't believe I had found it.

If anyone saw the black folded cloth-like fanny pack, they probably thought like I did, that it was a mask. I got into the car and put the pack securely in my suitcase. I wasn't taking any more chances.

As I drove towards Utah, I was reminded by my angels that mercury was in retrograde. Retrogrades are a sign to take your time and slow down. Going back and retracing my steps was an important message.

When I was able to get a phone signal, I called my daughter to share what happened and to let her know I was going to be late meeting her. I took my time driving and continued thanking my angels along the way. I felt like they were reminding me of my intuition at the gas station.

My thought at that time was questioning if the inside pocket of my jacket was a pocket. It turned out it wasn't a pocket. The message to go towards the police station helped me to retrace my steps.

This experience was a reminder to me to slow down and pay close attention to my thoughts. This was my intuition assisting me.

> It's worth stopping for a moment, taking a breath, and checking in with yourself to see if one of your thoughts should be investigated further or other action taken.

## CHAPTER 42

# Spirit Appearing in My Room

One of my friends was having cardiac symptoms, due to long COVID, which she contracted a year ago. She was having cardiac surgery and stents put in. My friend asked if I could stay with her at home following her surgery. I stayed with her overnight to make sure everything was okay.

Later that morning, my friend said she was feeling better and thought I didn't need to stay the full day. I went home with the stipulation that if she didn't feel well, she would call me right away.

Later that afternoon, I received an urgent text from her, sharing that she was having difficulty breathing. I told her to call an ambulance, but she refused to call. She said she was waiting to hear back from her doctor.

I told her I was jumping into my car, but if she needed an ambulance sooner to call. I made it to her house in about fifteen minutes. She got into my car, and we headed straight to the emergency room. I dropped her off and waited nearby.

She texted me and said it was going to be a while, so I should go home and that she would keep me informed of her status.

At 9:30 p.m., she texted me to say that they were trying to get her blood pressure down, because it was dangerously high. I let her know that I had my phone with me, so if they released her tonight to call or text me and I would drive her home.

At 12:30 a.m., I woke up to my friend's spirit walking around my room, trying to turn a light on. I saw her spirit walk around to the other side of my bed. Surprisingly, I also saw my dog, Oliver, a big labradoodle, who had passed away four years ago. I could see him curled up where my pillows were next to me. He began barking at my friend very loudly.

I was told by various mediums in the past, those who are like me that have the gift of seeing Spirit, that there is always a big white dog with me. I knew this dog was Oliver. As soon as he barked, my friend disappeared.

Less than a minute later, I received a text from my friend saying she was being released and that she was being "put on a short leash." I couldn't believe that she used that phrase.

She proceeded to say that they called an Uber for her, so I didn't need to pick her up. She shared that she was feeling much better, and that they were able to lower her blood pressure. She felt good about going home and would text me in the morning.

I waited until mid-morning to call her again. My friend said she got some sleep and was feeling much better. I wanted to tell her about seeing her last night, but didn't know how to approach it.

I decided to just ask her, if she felt she had left her body while at the hospital. She said she was so out of it, because they were having a challenge controlling her high blood pressure that she didn't know.

Personally, I wondered if she was close to death with her blood pressure so out of control and proceeded to share seeing her in my room. She was shocked. I even mentioned to her that the wording she used when she told me they were releasing her, but only on a short leash led me to wonder if on some level, she did see my dog.

I proceeded to tell her that Oliver, my dog was in the room, too and barked at her. His barking helped signal to her to get back into her body immediately. She was amazed and so was I.

## CHAPTER 43

# 2 ETs in My Back Seat

My friend and I went to the Grand Canyon for the day. Driving back home is always beautiful, especially with the colorful desert sky. However, this trip driving home was quite unique.

We noticed a huge cloud that spanned across the sky. It looked like a gigantic object that was being hidden in the clouds as if cloaked. We both instantly said, "That's a huge spaceship." We shared information about seeing similar cloaked ships in the clouds in the past. Then we shifted our conversation onto other subjects.

As we were driving through the canyon from Flagstaff to Sedona, suddenly I felt the presence of two ETs in our back seat. My friend asked, "Do you feel something odd?"

I responded, "Yes, there are two ETs in the back seat—I can feel them." One thing I knew was that they were benevolent. In my vision, through my third eye, they were small in stature.

My friend asked if they had a message for us. I felt their presence was confirmation that they were from the ship that we had seen in the huge cloud. Their visit was brief, so after a few minutes, we felt they were gone.

When I dropped my friend off at her home she said, "Let me know if you get any messages in your dreams from them."

I responded, "You too," and then I left.

During the night, I woke up to the same two ETs from my car. They were now in my bedroom. They were on the side of my bed looking at me in anticipation. I felt as if they were holding my covers in their hands anxiously waiting for me to wake up. It was the same feeling I got when I was a kid and was so excited on Christmas morning waiting for our parents to hurry up and get out of bed so we could open our presents.

The message that they were transmitting to me telepathically was that they were helping humanity with ascension. They are here to help us in remembering who we truly are. Symbolically waiting for me to wake up is like anxiously waiting for humanity to wake up.

In essence, the message revealed that I was waking up, as we are all waking up, by raising our frequency. Collectively, ascension is happening within all on earth. These beings are able to meet us at our own frequencies now, because we as a group have raised our frequency.

> They were there to confirm ascension was taking place within humanity, and we have help.

CHAPTER 44

# My White Jeep

It's Saturday and my friend and I decided to go to Pine, Arizona. I had never been there and we thought it would be fun. I met her at Camp Verde and we drove together.

On the way, we talked about what was going on in each other's lives. It wasn't until about halfway there that she mentioned something that seemed odd. She asked, "Have you noticed all the white cars on the road?"

I was thinking the same thing. As we spoke about it, there we saw one in front of us, one in back, and one driving by. Then three more went by us. This continued the entire trip. We were both wondering what was the significance of all these white cars.

When we arrived at Pine, which is a quaint little town, we discovered an herbal shop. We had fun buying teas for ourselves and gifts for others. I even bought a Unicorn tea. There's always room for miracles and magic.

After shopping, we went to lunch and headed home. Sure enough, the same thing happened—we saw white cars everywhere. Now if you've ever visited or lived in Sedona, you'll know that having a white car isn't the best idea, because of all the red rock dirt.

While my friend was driving, I decided to check in with Spirit and do a card reading. The message I got was loud and clear. There is a new level of angels here on earth to help humanity.

When my friend dropped me off at my car, she asked me to let her know if I continued to see white cars on the way back to my house. I agreed and asked her to do the same and then I left.

Sure enough, while driving I was surrounded by white cars. *This is wild*, I thought, but it didn't stop there. During the week, I resumed offering my meditations online.

I had taken a break, but was nudged by Spirit to begin again. I wanted to introduce a series on manifesting with the new earth energies. It was time to put these energies to work in my personal life, too.

What am I going to manifest? Immediately a picture of a Jeep popped into my head. I've always wanted one, but never pursued it. I love my purple Cosmic Cruiser—she's the best, but I can't go off-road with her in Sedona.

When teaching my manifesting class, I have participants visualize and feel as if it's already appeared in their physical reality. Now it's time to practice what I teach.

I went online to look at a Jeep dealership. I was thinking, what color would I like—maybe army green or blue? When looking at the colors, the page immediately went to a white Jeep.

I looked and thought, *I really don't want a white one,* so I hit the Back button to have more color choices. The page automatically changed back to a white Jeep.

I wondered what was happening, but I thought this must be Spirit telling me to get a white Jeep, so I surrendered. The next day I drove to West Sedona and I noticed that my manifesting shifted from white cars to white Jeeps. There were so many white Jeeps on the road while driving that it was overwhelming.

I called my friend to tell her how the massive number of white cars turned into white Jeeps. I also told my story about white cars and jeeps to class participants. After sharing this, many of them said they had been seeing them, too.

# THIS IS A VERY IMPORTANT LIFETIME FOR YOU

A couple of weeks later, I saw an ad for a used white Jeep. I knew I had to go see it. I was prompted by two almost accidents in my cruiser. I was getting the feeling that I was being nudged by my angels to go see this Jeep.

The signs kept coming. I was getting into the cruiser after hiking with one of my hiking friends. While backing out, I saw a white Jeep with a black soft top like the one I planned on going to see.

I drove to the dealership to check out the white Jeep. I hesitate to talk to car salespeople, because I feel like I'm being pressured to buy. I asked Spirit to help me not be seen by car salespeople, so I could see the Jeep on my own. I parked in front and several car sales people were standing there. I walked right by them and over to the side parking lot. I couldn't see the Jeep anywhere.

Ten minutes later, a young man came out of the building and asked if he could help. He asked if I was looking for something special. I shared with him that I saw an ad for a used Jeep.

He knew exactly which one and told me it was in a different lot, so he took me to see it. When we pulled up, I became excited and started negotiations immediately. I traded my beautiful faithful Cosmic Cruiser and now am the proud owner of a white Jeep.

The young salesperson was curious as to what I did for a living. I told him I had been a school nurse working with children who had learning challenges. He told me that he himself had learning challenges.

He asked more questions and I revealed that I was a holistic reader and healer. He excitedly took something out of his pocket to show me. It was a beautiful crystal. We looked at each other knowing this was divinely orchestrated.

I was his first sale. He needed the sale and I personally was on a mission to find the white Jeep to which the angels guided me. Before I left, he said he had to ask me something. "How did you get by all those car salespeople?"

I told him, "I cloaked myself energetically so they wouldn't see me."

He smiled as if to understand and said, "I'm so glad you did."

---

> The angels are reminding us that we have the power to manifest. We can manifest anything with intent. For me it was the white Jeep and being invisible to car sales people. What would you like to manifest in your life at this time?

# CHAPTER 45

# Archangel Michael, Blue Angels, and a Visit with Bigfoot

I have never seen this before. As I was driving, I noticed a reddish strand of hair on my right forearm about an inch long. I showed my friend who was in the front passenger seat. My hair is blonde. Where did this red hair come from? Perplexed, we both laughed about it. This was on November 10, 2021.

That night I was awakened by a visit from Archangel Michael and a team of Blue Angels. They were working on strengthening me. I could see shimmering blue light and was telepathically informed who it was. I could feel them working on the base of my spine, my root chakra.

Whenever I feel Spirit working on me, either physically, emotionally, mentally, or spiritually, I always command, "If this isn't for my highest good, then Go Now—I do not give consent," I then say, "If it is for my highest good, you may stay."

During this experience I felt such peace, love, and gratitude, I knew this was from the Divine. They were helping me by strengthening my foundation. I put my head back down on my pillow, took a deep breath, and closed my eyes. I allowed this beautiful healing to take place.

It was after this healing visit that I quickly went into a lucid dream. It's now November 11th. I was quickly transported to a forest and I was standing out in the middle of it. About two feet in front of my face was the feeling of pure unconditional love. I could see love emanating from his eyes. It was the face of an ape—it was Bigfoot. I wasn't scared, as he was pure love. I was in the dream, but also outside of it, looking in as an observer. This happens to me a lot.

I was so excited and filled with the love that was pouring out from this being in front of me. I was encompassed especially by the love pouring from his soulful eyes. It could have been God. That's the love that was emanating from this being. He had layered reddish brown hair and each strand was about an inch long. It was beautifully layered. His eyes were sparkling, with long eyelashes. Two other Bigfoot beings were on either side of his shoulders.

To my surprise, next, I noticed a small head that had no body. I asked Bigfoot, "What happened?"

He telepathically said that they are being hunted. I felt an overwhelming sadness for them. How could anyone hunt these beautiful souls?

Then I woke up. I immediately drew what he looked like. Then I made the connection to the single red hair on my wrist earlier that day in the car. I felt so much love when I woke up that I kept saying to myself, "Oh, my God, they are beings of pure love, so how could this happen to them?

I've never really given Bigfoot much thought. I have a close friend, who loves to research Bigfoot. As a matter of fact, she was driving with me earlier that day. I immediately called her and shared my experiences.

She began sending me videos of Bigfoot sightings and information. I watched one and shut it off. Humans have villainized these beautiful beings.

Later that day I spoke with a friend who is a healer. She said that Bigfoot can transport anywhere, because they are multidimensional beings. She also said that they come to you when they want to work with you.

I am great-full for the connection with Bigfoot, but I wasn't sure what to expect after that. I just felt more love in my heart when thinking about Bigfoot.

It was Monday, November 15th. A good friend was meeting me in West Sedona to hike a trail in the canyon. We met up early with the intention of going to the Birthing Cave.

The hiking trails there are tricky and sure enough, we got on the wrong trail. I asked her if she wanted to turn around, but she said that we should keep going.

She's one to trust and go with the flow, so we stayed on the trail we were on. We hiked a long way in. No one else was on the trail with us. We were in solitude with beautiful nature. As we made our way toward the end of the trail, we came to beautiful red rock formations.

There was a cave high above us. My friend commented on how it looked like Buddha. So we decided this was a good place to sit and do a meditation. Our intention was to bridge a sense of peace and healing between ancient civilizations and us.

As we sat on two rocks side by side, we quietly settled into silence. After a few minutes of silence, we were startled by a loud screeching sound.

Looking at each other in disbelief, I wondered if we both had heard the same screeching sound. We sat there completely still, so it was obvious we both heard it. I thought of videoing the area so I could capture this unusual sound, which had lasted about a minute.

I was so excited I recorded what we were hearing. Shortly after the screeching sound stopped, we ended our meditation. As we stood up facing each other, I saw a large tall being quickly walking through the trees out of my peripheral vision. I couldn't believe what I was seeing. I knew it was Bigfoot. I said out loud, "That's Bigfoot!" My friend agreed with me.

The hair on the back of my neck was standing straight up. We had Goddess bumps all over.

I thought, *It's him!*

Earlier I had shared with her my two dream visits with Archangel Michael and Bigfoot on November 11th. As it happened, she is now a part of this story.

We decided it was time to turn around and head back on the trail. I remembered hearing that Bigfoot liked to receive gifts. We wanted to leave a gift. Knowing it's dry in the canyon; I thought water would be a good gift. We looked around and found a cactus that was in the shape of a bowl. I poured the water in and yelled out, "We left you water here."

Then, I thought, *We can leave him a peanut butter bar, too.*

I had one left in my backpack. The question was, where should I leave it so Bigfoot will find it?

We walked back along the path in the direction of our car. I continued to look for a place to leave the water and the bar. We had a long hike back to the car. My friend was saying she felt like she had a veil around her. She could feel the veil slowly lifting as we continued to walk towards the car.

Were we in a different dimension? As we walked back on the same path that we had originally taken into the canyon, we saw a woman's black sun hat lying upside down in the middle of the path.

We both looked at each other. How did this get here? We hadn't seen a soul on this path. We would have come across anyone and the hat on our way into the canyon. Maybe it was a sign to leave the water and the bar here for Bigfoot.

# THIS IS A VERY IMPORTANT LIFETIME FOR YOU

I yelled out again, "We left water and a peanut butter bar for you!" We both giggled and kept walking. As we continued, the veil totally lifted from my friend. We both sensed that Bigfoot was gone.

We were excited to listen to the video recordings, especially the second one. As I played the first video recording, there was video footage of the forest. I had taken the video when we first arrived along with photos.

I checked the original clip of the area, which was about twenty seconds long and had sound. The second one, a fifty-second clip of the screeching sound had completely disappeared.

This seemed strange, so I wondered what happened to it. After sharing our disappointment about the missing sound, we realized it made sense. We were in another density, another dimension with Bigfoot.

The screeching sounds we heard in the canyon were identical to the sounds on the Bigfoot videos that my other friend sent to me after I shared my dream. Our Bigfoot encounter was real.

When I later looked at the photos of the red rock formations, I noticed there was a clear image of an ape-shaped head. Have others been as privileged as we were that day to see Bigfoot? Life sure is getting more and more interesting every day.

Thank you, Bigfoot, AA Michael,
and The Blue Angels.

## CHAPTER 46

# Tall Gray Stone Beings

I guess I'm moving to the ocean, or in my case, it would be the Gulf. This was my thought upon waking from my dream.

First, I'll start with the back story. I had just returned from visiting my son in California. Before going to bed, I had a few things on my mind. The first was getting my taillight cover repaired, as I almost had an accident on the freeway in California.

I was about fifteen minutes before arriving to his home. When I travel, I always ask the angels to surround and protect me, my vehicle, and everyone else around me, including animals, birds—you name it. I am great~full I did.

It seemed everyone was in a hurry and speeding. I had someone riding my bumper for several miles. Why do people do that? I would brake, every now and then just to have the car behind me give some space, in case I needed to stop.

Suddenly everything came to a screeching halt in front of me. I looked into my rear-view mirror and the car behind me that was riding my bumper was coming at me full force. I didn't think he could stop, so I put my hand up in the mirror to draw attention for him to stop.

He came to within an inch from my bumper. I was relieved I wasn't hit—I'm okay. However, it was a different story for the man behind me and the three behind him. They all hit like dominoes. I was visibly shaken by this.

Fortunately, it wasn't serious as everyone slid into the person in front of them without too much damage. I thanked my angels for protecting me. I called my son to share what had happened and then proceeded to make it safely to his home.

We looked at the bumper together, and there wasn't even a scratch on it. The only thing was a taillight cover that fell to the ground when we inspected it. It must have been the air impact that loosened it. I put the light cover in the car to fix when I return to Sedona.

We had a wonderful visit for the weekend, and I drove safely back to Sedona. However, I was exhausted after driving, so fell asleep right away that night.

In dreamtime, I was standing at the beach shoreline facing what looked like the Florida Gulf. My hands are in prayer position at my heart. Right before my eyes, tall gray stone beings rose out of the water and formed a circle. I stood and completed the circle. The stone formation looked like Stonehenge or pictures of what Atlantis would look like.

I asked the tall gray stone beings if I could join them. I repeated the phrase, "May I join you—may I join you?" Then I woke up.

This felt like more than a dream, so I knew I was there. I thought to myself, *I'm moving to the water*. I didn't know exactly when this would happen. I wasn't in a rush, as I loved living in Sedona.

However, my heart knew it was time, as I had completed my divine purpose here. The energy of Sedona allows me to go within and be in nature while hiking in the red rock. My work involved offering meditations, Reiki sessions, and readings, but I knew there was more to be accomplished.

The past three years in Sedona were about fulfilling a dream, living more in the moment, and working on myself while also helping others. I went for my morning hike and meditation on the Red Rock and brought my dream journal. After meditating on the mountain, I intuitively received a message to check my email. There was an email from the woman from whom I leased my home.

I couldn't believe what I was reading. She informed me that my lease was not going to be renewed. I had hoped I would be here for another year. Spirit was preparing me, using dreamtime to show that the water was calling. My time in Sedona was coming to an end.

However, it wasn't until I saw a YouTube video the following month that I knew Spirit in Dreamtime was telling me something. The video was Jason Shurka interviewing Dr. Sandra Rose Michael about the Energy Enhancement System she invented.

This was it—I was being called to a higher purpose. Could this be near water like in my dream? I called my sister who lived in Florida and told her to watch this interesting video.

After watching the video, I knew in my heart that I was supposed to be doing a healing center in Florida with my sister. Initially, she wasn't sure. Each day she would go back and forth on whether to get involved or not.

A close family member had just been diagnosed with leukemia. My sister was researching to see if this EESystem could benefit them. She couldn't find any information prior to falling asleep. That night she had a spiritual experience.

In the middle of the night, she was shaken awake. She looked around and saw her husband sleeping soundly. She noticed her computer was open and saw on the screen a physician's research describing how the EESystem has helped his patients with leukemia. This was her sign, so now she was definitely in.

It was the day she said, "I'm in" that I got the name for our center, "SoulfulWaves," I knew this was the perfect name and my sister agreed. The ball was now in motion. I booked movers and spent the next couple of months packing up my home and saying goodbye to my beloved Sedona.

I remembered an angel reading I had in April. It was after my Stone Beings dream, but before knowing about the EESystem. The angel reader saw a wellness center. He kept saying, "The angels want you to go BIG, not small, go Big." He also saw people crawling on a beach who were very ill coming to the center. I didn't put it together until later. It all made sense.

A month later, we found the perfect spot for our center. Our EESystem was installed shortly after. The energy was palpable. Our anticipation was over, and we are now in the midst of fulfilling our mission.

The three years in Sedona helped prepare me for this next part of my journey to the Gulf of Florida. This was the water in my dream. It wasn't until two weeks after opening our doors that I realized Spirit guided this whole mission.

I remember, I was standing in the middle of our EESystem room when I shared my dream with a client. I told him about the tall gray stone beings and at that moment, it was Eureka!

I turned around and said, "It's them, look at the four EESystem racks. They are the tall gray stone beings that rose out of the water."

The dream's impact got the ball rolling with the lease ending, the video appearing, the discussion with my sister about the EESystem, the move close to the water, the name received in meditation, and the opening of the wellness center showing all the synchronicities. Everything has come full circle and is complete.

# CHAPTER 47

# A School Teacher, a Student, and a Tornado

I scheduled a session with a woman who specializes in identifying past lives and offers energy healing. In one of the lifetimes she revealed to me, I was a female school teacher.

She shared that I taught in a single-building school, where all the children were in one class together. One day before lunch, the weather looked like a tornado was forming. Since the tornado was imminent, I needed to get the children to safety, but I had to do this in groups.

It was when I returned to the classroom, after taking the remainder of the group to safety, I saw there was one more child left, who was terrified. I picked her up and wrapped her in my arms, just as the tornado hit us.

I was so close to getting this little girl to safety when I was struck down and died. I thought she perished with me and that I failed to save her. I died with the feelings of heavy guilt in my heart. What I didn't know was that she lived. I had saved her.

This past life trauma was not for me to carry into the next lifetime. As the reader was speaking, I felt overwhelmed with emotion. This all rang true for me. I felt a huge release of emotions knowing this truth.

In 2022 my sister and I co-founded SoulfulWaves, an Energy Enhancement Center. It was a few months after opening when I received a call from a mother who was bringing two of her children to the center. One daughter was nine years old and her sister was six.

Their mom had told me that there was a lot going on in their lives. Her oldest daughter was very sensitive and the youngest had difficulties focusing and sitting still. The mom said she didn't want to disturb others in the session since it was a group session with other people. She said if her younger daughter was challenged sitting still in the session, she would take her outside.

When the mom and the girls came into the center, the oldest daughter looked around and immediately said she knew this place. She then leaned over and whispered to her Mom, "I know her from a past life."

Her mom repeated what her daughter had said and immediately we all had goosebumps. It was after their session when I found out that the youngest daughter slept the entire time. She was the one that the mom was concerned wouldn't be able to sit still.

When they came out of the session, they were very animated. We all had fun looking at the gifts that were on display. It was right before they were leaving when the oldest daughter ran up to me and wrapped her arms around me. She wouldn't let go of me. Tears rolled down my face as I hugged her back.

We looked into each other's eyes. There was a knowingness between us. The oldest daughter didn't want to leave my side and I felt the same way. My heart strings were being pulled. It was getting late and they needed to get on the road to go home. The mom informed the girls that they would be back again soon.

Later that evening I met friends for dinner. We weren't sure we were going to meet, as there was a tornado warning. It was very blustery, but we decided to meet anyway. I was happy, because I needed to tell them what happened that evening. Without sharing names, I told them about the mother and her daughters who visited the center. I shared what an amazing experience it was and how the daughter recognized me, even though we had never met before.

The next morning, I was urged by Spirit to write about my past lives, especially the one as the school teacher when I was trying to save the children in the tornado. I immediately received confirmation that the oldest daughter from yesterday, who said she knew me in a past life, was the little girl I had saved in the schoolhouse. In that past life together, I thought she had died in the tornado.

Later that day, I was sharing this added connection I made with my friend who was at dinner with us the night before. We were sitting around her pool. It was a calm day up until I shared the story about the schoolhouse and the tornado.

Suddenly, we heard loud swirling wind sounds come out of nowhere. This was more confirmation that the little girl from the schoolhouse was the oldest daughter that came with her mom to our center yesterday. The tornado from the previous night along with meeting the oldest daughter triggered a remembering.

Here are my thoughts:

I thought the little school girl had died in the tornado, so I held onto that grief when I died. When the oldest daughter saw me at the center in this lifetime, on an intuitive level, she knew I was the schoolteacher who had saved her. She must have thought in the past lifetime that I had died saving her and was gone forever. The way she held on to me so tightly at the center was a deep remembering of our connection on a soul level.

This experience provided deep healing for us. The Universe is amazing how it brings us together with our soul groups. I hope to see this family again, especially the oldest daughter. Thank you, Spirit.

## ABOUT THE AUTHOR

Nancy Adele is a Registered Nurse and holds a BSN from Boston College. She specializes in Integrative Therapies. As a Reiki Master Teacher, Channel, and Intuitive Reader Nancy has been practicing for over 25 years. She founded the IAM Wellbeing Healing Center in Stoughton, Massachusetts where she focused on the application of vibrational sciences, meditation, and wellness programs for her clients. Through her IAM Wellbeing Healing Center Nancy contracted with medical facilities such as Dana Farber/Brigham and Women's Hospital Cancer Center in Milford; Shields Radiation Oncology Center in Mansfield and South Suburban Oncology Center in Quincy providing Integrative Healing Services, such as Reiki, Chi-Gong, meditation, and relaxation therapies for patients undergoing treatment for cancer. After eight years Nancy moved her IAM Wellbeing Healing Center to Sedona, AZ. Three years later Nancy was called to Sarasota, FL. Sedona, AZ. had prepared her energetically to expand her Wellness Center once again in Sarasota, Florida. Nancy is the Co-Founder of Sarasota's SoulfulWaves, a Humanity-Focused Energy Enhancement Healing Center with her sister Joy. For more information about Nancy Adele and SoulfulWaves or to book an appointment go to:*www.soulfulwaves.com*.

Printed in the USA
CPSIA information can be obtained
at www.ICGtesting.com
CBHW032254060724
11149CB00012B/650